"I had three chairs in
my house: one for solitude,
two for friendship, three
for society."

HENRY DAVID THOREAU, *Walden*

CHIC
SIMPLE

HOME

ALFRED A. KNOPF   NEW YORK   1993

THIS IS A BORZOI BOOK
PUBLISHED BY ALFRED A. KNOPF, INC.

KIM JOHNSON GROSS   JEFF STONE
WRITTEN BY JULIE V. IOVINE
PHOTOGRAPHS BY MARIA ROBLEDO
ILLUSTRATIONS BY ERIC HANSON

STYLED BY FRITZ KARCH

DESIGN AND ART DIRECTION BY ROBERT VALENTINE INCORPORATED

Library of Congress Cataloging-in-Publication Data
Iovine, Julie V. [date]
Home/written by Julie V. Iovine; photographs, Maria Robledo
p. cm.—(Chic simple)
ISBN 0-679-42167-X
1. Interior decoration—United States—History—20th century.
I. Title. II. Series.
NK2004.W67 1993
747.213'09'049—dc20
92-54807
CIP

Manufactured in the United States of America
First Edition

"The more you know, the less you need."

AUSTRALIAN ABORIGINAL
SAYING

CONTENTS

CHIC
CHIC
SIMPLE

Chic Simple is a primer for living well but sensibly in the 1990s. The desire for a quality of life that is defined not by the accumulation of things but rather by a paring down to the best essentials—with a commitment to home, community, and environment. In a world of limited natural resources, Chic Simple enables readers to bring value and style into their lives with economy and simplicity.

FOUNDATION

No matter what label-making pundits might say, there is no one life-style that dictates the look of a particular era. ♟ The Deco curves that define the Thirties originated in the Twenties and the Teens. ♟ The symbolic tie-dye of the Sixties really flowered in the Seventies. And so it goes. Many factors—economic, cultural, material, sociological—influence the spirit of life-style. ♟ And yet, over a span of years, sensibilities and attitudes shift and reactions set in against the taste of a previous time. The accumulated effect is that we do ascribe certain set images to specific epochs. If only to illuminate where we're going, it helps to cast an eye back on where we've been. ♟

'30s

EVENTS:

Stock Market Crash and the opening of the Museum of Modern Art
in New York, both in 1929; Chicago World's Fair of 1933

STYLES: Art Deco, Modernism, Gothic Tudor

PRODUCT: totalitarian governments

MATERIALS: black lacquer, chrome

SHAPES: curved, rectilinear

ROOM: the lounge

THIS ERA FOREVER TRAPPED

BETWEEN TWO WORLD WARS IS FRAUGHT WITH CONTRADICTIONS: THE PARALYSIS OF THE DEPRESSION VERSUS BURSTING CREATIVE ENERGIES AND then preparation for war. The seductive curve of Art Deco, already made famous at the International Exposition of Decorative Arts and Industrial Modernism in Paris, 1925, was quickly absorbed by the mainstream and resulted in high-style Luxe and, ultimately, Populuxe. The most exquisite examples of Art Deco were often by such French craftsman-designers as Émile-Jacques Ruhlmann, who reveled in the use of exotic materials: sharkskin, black lacquer, and mother-of-pearl inlays. Deco worked well with metal chrome, and its swoop and swank was the perfect metaphor for the energy and dash promised by the new technologies of aerodynamic design just then appearing. Soon, every lamp shade, coffeepot, and vacuum cleaner had a streamlined profile. While the first wave of Art Deco played itself out in the Thirties, Modernism was just on the rise. The principles of Modernism—design that is functional, mass-producible, stripped of excess and ornament—were already well known in Europe. The Bauhaus was founded in 1919; and Mies van der Rohe's celebrated Barcelona Pavilion opened in 1929. It took many more years for Modernism to establish itself in the United States. Public buildings adapted the style more readily than residential architecture, which still favored a pastiche of period looks. The Museum of Modern Art's International Style show in 1932 was instrumental in exhibiting Modernist buildings to the intelligentsia; but it was through Hollywood movies, where the graceful nonchalance of a Fred Astaire spin was played out against a backdrop of elegant Deco-influenced Modernism, that the larger public got its first convincing glance at the style that would dominate the next five decades.

'40 $_s$

IN AMERICA,

THE POSTWAR FORTIES

WERE SHAPED BY THE

exuberant energy of a victorious

nation emerging after 1945 in

control of more than half the

world's export trade. Industrial

designers Charles and Ray

Eames explored the advantages

of molded plywood and were

among the first to achieve truly

EVENT:
the end of W.W.II

STYLE:
Modernism—crisp,
reductive, geometric
along with
streamlining derived
from aerodynamic
engineering and
transportation
design.

PRODUCT:
Charles and Ray
Eames DCW side
chair, 1946

MATERIAL:
molded plywood

SHAPE:
right angles and the
bullet or teardrop taper

ROOM:
all-glass living room
and patio

mass-producible furniture with their famous plywood DCW chair. The immigration of most of the exponents of European Modernism to the United States —Walter Gropius, Ludwig Mies van der Rohe, Marcel Breuer, and Laszlo Moholy-Nagy—meant the Modernist notion that form follows function soon helped substantiate a fast-paced building boom that hadn't the time to construct anything but structures that were streamlined, free of ornament, and structurally exposed.

After the war, reunited families were dissatisfied with ritual-bound traditions of the past. They sought a more contemporary sensibility fueled by the 1933 House of Tomorrow. Interior design tended toward crisp minimalism with solid panels of color or occasional geometric patterns. With the victorious mood came social responsibility: a prime example was the influential Case Study houses program sponsored by *Arts and Architecture* magazine in 1945 that sought to design affordable houses for a burgeoning class of postwar middle-class newlyweds. Two years later, developer William J. Levitt was selling $6,900 houses in Long Island at a rate of 150 a week. Levittown and the new world of the suburbs were born.

THE ATOMIC
AGE OF THE FIFTIES SAW STYLE MASS-PRODUCED ALONG WITH

the conviction that high-quality goods were meant for everybody. The baby boom was well under way; and the new suburbia was a mobile society needing interstate highways, drive-in restaurants, and the Cadillac.

After the testing of bombs in Nevada, the launching of Sputniks I and II in 1957, and the discovery of the helix structure of DNA in 1953, scientific imagery began leaving its own indelible mark on design: atoms, mushroom clouds, and helixes were used as upbeat decorative motifs on everything from clocks to fabrics. Biomorphic and asymmetrical shapes already visible in the art of Joan Miró, Alexander Calder, and Henry Moore translated into kidney-shaped cocktail tables and swimming pools, boomerang patterns, teardrop-shaped vacuum cleaners, and automobile tail fins.

At home the two-child, commuting-husband-and-housewife family unit had a rec-room with a new television set. White interiors accented in primary colors or black carried on the Modernist legacy with pared-down Scandinavian imports or modular seating as furniture. The appearance of synthetic plastics, fiberglass, and laminates such as Formica were applauded for their easy maintenance and no-wear toughness. The zeitgeist was all optimism and opportunity. With Doris Day in the movies, Disneyland opening in California, and McDonald's serving its first burger in Illinois, the joys of artifice were well on the way to supplanting more authentic values.

EVENT:
neutron bomb testing in Nevada; McCarthy trials

STYLE:
organic Modernism

PRODUCT:
Philco television sets

MATERIAL:
Formica

SHAPE:
biomorphic

ROOM:
rec-room

'50s

Of all the revolutions that occurred in the Sixties—personal, sexual, political—the style revolution was one of the most subtly subversive. Modernism's own radical roots were largely forgotten. In a crescendo of rock music and folk-song laments, the new generation rejected the prosperity of the suburbs and set out for the liberation of raw experience. Anti-style was the new look of the anti-hero; and pop culture supplied the lingo of a new vision. Non-judgment, if not exactly equality, became the standard of value in home decor. Psychedelic and pop palettes entered the living room through both high-end Italian furniture and off the street. Marble and laminates, natural fibers and synthetic fabrics existed side by side. To Mies van der Rohe's famous "Less is more," architect Robert Venturi retorted "Less is a bore" in his landmark essays *Complexity and Contradiction* (1966) and *Learning from Las Vegas* (1972).

In a further reaction against the depersonalizing effects of standardization, furniture tended toward the idiosyncratic and the outrageous. Eero Saarinen's Womb and the Bean Bag chair are high and low inventions of the Sixties. Quaint as these designs seem to us now, they imparted an invaluable legacy of wit, energy, and personality that remain the essential ingredients of good design in any age.

sixties

EVENT: Kennedy's assassination, Woodstock   **STYLE:** psychedelic, pop à la Milton Glaser graphics

PRODUCT: Bean Bag chair   **MATERIAL:** natural fibers   **SHAPE:** inflated   **ROOM:** sunken living room

seventies

With the early years still caught up in the revolutionary thrall of the Sixties, the Seventies were the decade that style forgot: who remembers supergraphics, macramé planters, Indian prints, shag rugs, and chrome and glass étagères? Life-styles were shaped by women's liberation, sexual experimentation, and Watergate, not design. With jogging, the wok, and *The Joy of Sex*, this was the decade that turned inward and got personal. By 1975, Tom Wolfe had already dubbed the seventies the "Me decade." At home, the raw "found objects" that furnished the Sixties gave way to High Tech, a look that borrowed its imagery and materials (especially chrome) from industrial sources and from Europe. Aeronautical runway lights lit the kitchen or a photographer's umbrella added mood to the master bedroom. The domestic palette ranged from earth-tone browns and forest greens accented with pop touches in orange, red, and yellow to highly lacquered red or black.

College students and young couples were the dominant force in defining life-style. Recycling was, first, a resourceful way to save money and, second, an anti-establishment aesthetic. Orange crates became bookshelves. And yet, it is to this decade with its passion for the "natural" that the first stirrings of environmental concern can be traced. While "organic" in the Fifties had meant biologically inspired shapes, now it related to biodegradable content. In the Seventies, Knoll International introduced the first ergonometric office chair, and the term "global warming" surfaced in the mass media.

EVENT: Watergate, the energy crisis **STYLE:** Nature's Way and High Tech **PRODUCT:** furniture systems
MATERIAL: Indian prints, fiber wall hangings **SHAPE:** supergraphics **ROOM:** bedroom

Postmodernism supplanted Modernism and, while the debate raged, architects could stake their careers on the design of a well-turned column. Historical references and wit were in; pure function, out. The construction business boomed and newly dramatic skylines appeared on the horizon of every mid-size American town. A new class of super-consumer emerged: yuppies. And their look was Euro-style, or else nineteenth-century English traditional. Two major trends—Italy and irony—converged in the furniture by Memphis noted for its pop colors, lopsided proportions, and humor. Price was not an

EVENT:
two terms of Ronald
Reagan as President

STYLE:
Postmodernism

'80s

PRODUCT:
Michael Graves's
teakettle

MATERIAL:
terra-cotta

SHAPE:
column

ROOM:
restaurants

issue. In 1984, the Italian manufacturer Alessi introduced architect Michael Graves's teakettle in a limited edition for $18,000. The basic vocabulary of Postmodernism was quickly adapted to the home, often in the form of classical moldings and oversize pediments. The energy of the Eighties was more about display than domesticity. We entertained in restaurants instead of our living rooms. With its predilection for distressed and gold-leaf surfaces, imported luxury appliances, and minimal lighting, the Eighties make an easy target. Still, it was a great decade for liberating imaginations and for reconnecting with the past.

'90s

THE PRESENT DECADE IS ONLY

JUST BEGINNING, BUT IT IS SHAPING UP AS A PERIOD OF TAKING STOCK AND ACCEPTING RESPONSIBILITY FOR OUR OWN LIVES AND THE LIFE OF THE PLANET. Today, the status of style has both a more complex and a simpler definition: labels are not enough. Good design means objects and spaces that have value because they work not only on a functional level but an emotional one as well. There is no New Look. More than ever, the home serves a nurturing role. In a world of shrinking resources, it has become the place for self-expression, for balance, for recycling, and for refueling. Consequently, it's a time for thinking smaller but also smarter about how to create personal environments. For, in spite of the so-called saving powers of technology, time itself seems to be shrinking. Mail-order catalogues and many design stores understand that in today's terms efficiency means access and authenticity. For a generation intent on reevaluating its role in the world, style today appreciates the resonance of simplicity.

SPACE

"If we were being genuinely honest we would have
to say that probably the most comfortable interior
environment ever invented is the middle-class suburban
home. In other words, comfort, physical comfort, is wall-
to-wall carpeting, lots of sofas and chairs, and
everything very clean."

FRAN LEBOWITZ

"Unlike sculpture and painting which produce
objects in space, buildings contain space. Moreover, it
is space that is intended not only to be experienced
and admired but also to be inhabited."

WITOLD RYBCZYNSKI
The Most Beautiful House in the World

Understanding space is the first step toward transforming it. Even a seemingly empty room is loaded with information. The most effective spaces are often not designed at all. They evolved over time and in response to need. The centuries-old rituals and philosophy that dictate the form of a tatami-lined tea house in Japan differ vastly from the religious considerations influencing the lines of a chair in a Shaker meeting hall. Similarly, the forces of nature and physics that decree the streamlined efficiency aboard a sailboat are hardly necessary on land. Different as these unique spaces are, they all share a beauty and an appropriateness that says, "Here, object and material serve well." It is from such vernacular and purpose-built spaces as these that the lessons in good design can best be learned.

Japanese

IN WESTERN CIVILI-ZATIONS, WALLS REP-RESENTED THE IDEA of shelter and the original foundations for supporting architecture. In Japan, the image of the roof dominates, and walls are little more than a thin membrane allowing free flow between the outdoors and the interior. Indeed, harmony with nature is the philosophy behind domestic architecture in Japan.

In the traditional Japanese home, there are three important areas, but no fixed enclosures. The most private part of the house, for sleeping and bathing, is at the center, not the back. Eating, socializing, and watching television all take place in the same space, which has no fixed furniture arrangements. Built-in shelves with sliding doors that look like walls contain what furniture there is: futons, tables, pillows. Thanks to the material richness of polished wood, woven tatami mats, exquisite textile hangings, and translucent white shoji screens, there is nothing bare about a traditional Japanese interior. A wide corridor or open verandah circles these living spaces, acting as an intermediate stage between interior and exterior. Extending from the roof, a deep overhang makes it possible to keep the house open but protected from bad weather. Folding shutters are the only "walls" separating the house from the garden, which is itself considered another room.

"A Japanese can make a whole life in a small space."
TADAO ANDO, *architect*

S h a k e r

THE SHAKERS WERE A RELIGIOUS SECT THAT BELIEVED THE beauty and perfection of heaven could be experienced by living simply and purely on earth. Shaker communities flourished in nineteenth-century America, spread over nineteen villages from Kentucky to Maine. At the height of their popularity there were as many as several thousand believers. Outsiders named them the "Shakers" because of the energetic dances they performed at religious meetings; they called themselves the "Society of Believers." For the Shakers, work, worship, and life were indivisible. They lived in self-sufficient communities where everything was shared and nearly everything handmade. Shaker objects are noted for their shapely simplicity, beautiful craftsmanship, and precise efficiency. In design, their furnishings are free of the unnecessary, but full of joy. Natural color —sky blue, ocher yellow, barn red, grass green—often saturates plain surfaces. The practical spirit of Shaker design is personable and idiosyncratic, not mechanical or automatic. Rocking chairs with a drawer under the seat, or a window inside a cupboard to let in light are typical commonsense solutions. The Shakers were not only pragmatic but inventive. We can thank them for the flat broom, clothespins, seed packets, circular saws, and swivel-footed chairs, to name just a few of the conveniences they introduced. The legacy of the Shakers shows how spiritual serenity combined with utilitarian sturdiness can produce designs of remarkable integrity and lasting pleasure.

SHAKER RULE OF THUMB
Don't make something unless it is both necessary and useful;
but if it is both necessary and useful, don't hesitate to make it beautiful.

Purpose-Built Design

BOATS, TRAINS, PLANES, AND AIRSTREAM TRAILERS ARE ALL MACHINES FROM WHICH INVALU-able design ideas for small spaces have been gathered. Mobility, compactness, durability, storage, and ventilation take priority. And yet these spaces often exercise over us the allure of romance associated with travel. Below deck on a sailboat, there's not an inch to spare. Galley, berth, and cabin are the only "rooms." Such spaces are either no bigger than necessary or designed to do double or sometimes triple duty. A storage bench by day folds out into a dining table or map-reading surface at other times. Shelves are all built-ins designed to prevent objects from flying loose at sea. Polished woodwork and brass fittings are not just luxuries but practical, durable materials that have withstood the test of time and hard wear. Here, style is function, and decor is craft.

"A house is a machine for living in."

LE CORBUSIER

The sleep spaces aboard a Boat or Train, even the bathrooms on an Airplane, are all classic instances of design that take maximum Advantage of the most minimal spaces and, in the process, produce some ingenious solutions in Compact Design.

"I told him I wanted a cross between a cell and a ship's cabin. I wanted my books in a corridor, and plenty of cupboards."

BRUCE CHATWIN

To his architect, John Pawson

DESIGN

AN EMPTY ROOM IS LOADED WITH MEANING, AND WITH POSSIBILITIES. THE PRINCIPLES OF

PRINCIPLES

DESIGN GOVERN THE LIFE OF THE SIMPLEST ROOM AND TRANSCEND ALL STYLE LABELS. WHEN WELL

OF

UNDERSTOOD AND JUDICIOUSLY APPLIED, THEY CAN TRANSFORM BLANK SPACE INTO A CHERISHED

DESIGN

ABODE. IN THIS CHAPTER, THE MOST BASIC BUILDING BLOCKS OF THE HOME ARE DEFINED.

SPACE: The first principle of architecture is space and how to set its limits in a way that expands our experience of openness rather than detracting from it. Accurately estimating the exact amount needed rather than simply requiring the maximum amount of space possible has become the most urgent requirement in the proper management of our personal environments. PROPORTION: Proportion is to architects what perspective is to painters: a way to create impressions far deeper and more experientially resonant than the physical world allows. Proportion is the geometry of space, and as such, its principles must be understood in order to take full advantage of the benefits it promises. LIGHT: Good lighting is a revelation. Through lighting—whether it is natural or artificial—the constant transformation of space is possible. The first step is to consider all the moods that come with the hours of the day in nature and then bring that richness to the interiors of the home. FUNCTION: Function is often deemed synonymous with modern design; and yet long before the American architect Louis Sullivan dictated that form should follow function, architects understood that function, in fact, has to do with many more operations than the merely mechanical. Emotional satisfaction is equally a function of good design. TEXTURE: In the most expanded sense of the word, texture defines the psychological depth of a room, its contrasts, and its richness of mood. Far more than the sum of the materials used to cover furniture, texture is about combining visual experiences with tactile ones. COLOR: Color requires confidence and caution. It makes an immediate and lasting impression on the eye. It is the easiest—and least costly—way to transform a room, and the most daring. Before splashing a room with color, remember that white is all colors blended in one and comes in its own wide range of shades. MEMORY & WIT: Few classic tomes would think to include memory and wit in their principles of design. And yet, in the world of today, where individual personality is often lost to mass-produced convenience, expression with a sense of humor and generosity is perhaps one of the most important *new* principles of contemporary design.

S p a c e

THE ENCLOSURE OF SPACE IS THE BEGINNING OF ALL ARCHITECTURE. TO SHAPE A SPACE FOR ONESELF—TO create a shelter—is to protect and encourage intimacy. Enclosed space is always in a subjective relationship to the landscape: either ignoring it or in harmony with it. Space can be manipulated, measured in real inches or else perceived by the eye alone. The spirit soars in a cathedral, cringes in a tunnel.

Imagine how high ceilings make you breathe more deeply and how small rooms seem inexplicably cozy. That's why architects will often suggest low ceilings at an entrance to maximize the experience of the space that stretches beyond. Similarly, when interior doors and openings are aligned to permit views to windows and the outside, the result is an impression of expansion. Even a chair simply arranged to look out a window captures an enlarged sense of space.

"Space and light and order. These are the things men need just as much as they need bread or a place to sleep."

LE CORBUSIER

L i g h t

LIKE PLANTS, PEOPLE—OR AT LEAST OUR MOODS—FLOUR- ISH IN DIRECT RELATIONSHIP to our exposure to natural light. Light and its opposite, shadow, work best when they modify space. Natural light entering through a variety of openings and windows with panes tends to be more evocative and stimulating than light through undefined plate glass. Artificial light is often necessary for a room to function properly. Diffused, or indirect, light establishes the emotional tone whether its source is natural or artificial. At home, that is the first layer of lighting required. So-called task lighting is the next step aimed at providing focused light. This too can be natural, although artificial light allows more flexibility. Whatever the source, remember that both layers—emotional and practical—combine in shedding the best light on a home's interior.

"If you can get the lighting right, many other things become less important, and you can actually have fewer things of better quality."

TERENCE CONRAN

VOICE OF WISDOM

Frank O. Gehry (b. 1929). Architect Frank O. Gehry first came to national attention in the Seventies as an aggressively idiosyncratic California architect who remodeled the walls of his own home with chain-link fencing. At a time when the country was sunk in economic depression, Gehry was, in fact, illustrating how the humblest materials—chain link, sheet metal, cardboard—could lead an inspiring life in architecture. He has since emerged as America's most original practicing architect who has managed to escape all attempts at aesthetic labeling. Rather than align himself with one of the contentious subsets of the contemporary architectural debate, Gehry has always preferred the company of artists, frequently collaborating with Claes Oldenburg, among others. His approach is intuitive, not theoretical; exploratory, not regimented. Gehry makes architecture that champions the complexity of materials and the energy of sculptural form. Repeatedly, Gehry has attracted notice as well for his experiments with furniture: first, the 1972 laminated cardboard "Easy Edges" series; then fish- and snake-shaped lamps; and, most recently, bentwood chairs for Knoll. Frank Gehry's work conveys his own contagious joy in the act of shaping the objects that populate and enrich our lives.

ICONS OF INFLUENCE

fish
snakes
cardboard
chain link
apple crates

"I believe creativity is a childlike activity and

SELECTED BUILDINGS

Gehry House, Los Angeles, 1979; Loyola Law School, Los Angeles, 1984; California Aerospace Museum, Los Angeles, 1984; Yale Psychiatric Institute, New Haven, Conn., 1989; Vitra Design Museum, Weil am Rhein, Germany, 1989; Chiat/Day Advertising Agency Headquarters, Los Angeles, 1992; American Center, Paris, France, 1994; Walt Disney Concert Hall, Los Angeles, 1996.

ARCHITECTURE

"Architecture should speak of its time and place, but
yearn for timelessness."

"I approach each building as a sculptural object,
a spatial container, a space with light and air, a
response to context and appropriateness of feeling
and spirit."

DESIGNING HOMES

"The images that compose your house can relate
to all kinds of symbolic things, ideas that you've liked,
places you've liked, bits and pieces of your life that
you would like to recall."

HIS APPROACH

"I want to be open-ended. There are no rules,
no right or wrong. I'm confused as to what's ugly and
what's beautiful."

to question too much may be irrelevant."

Proportion

PROPORTION IS THE RHYTHM OF A SPACE AND THE HARMONIOUS RELATIONSHIP OF ITS PARTS. THE height of the ceiling is in proportion to the width of the floor, the size of the windows and the doors. Proportion has been called music to the eye. In the past, symmetrical equivalence, where parts perfectly mirror each other, was the only acceptable proportion. Today, classical symmetry is not necessarily the point, although a pleasing sense of counterpoint and balance is still desirable. Proportion is about the geometry of lines and how they interact. And like jazz, proportions can be played with, repeated, and formalized for effect. Perfect symmetry, say two columns at an entrance or tall matching vases on a mantel, suggests formality.

On the other hand, exaggerated disproportion in the form of a massive bouquet of wildflowers in a delicate vase or tiny windows all in a row in a large room draws instant attention, perhaps a smile. Proportion allows you to adjust the scale between two objects or elements in order to accentuate or disguise their differences.

"It has been said that were I three inches taller than 5'8½", all my houses would have been quite different in proportion. Probably."

FRANK LLOYD WRIGHT

C o l o r

IF PROPORTION IS THE MUSIC OF SPACE, COLOR IS ITS POETRY. COLOR MAKES A ROOM COOL OR HOT, LARGE or small, inviting or formal. Even the subtlest hue when applied on all the walls will make a room feel smaller, warmer. On the other hand, painting moldings and trim white against off-white or any shade will make the architecture pop out. Don't forget that white is a color, with a full range of tones from pristine eggshell to dusky stucco. Color can bring a space to life, enrich its meaning through contrast and highlights. Coordinating a color scheme can be a complicated affair where everyone has an opinion. Learning the colors you like best by collecting samples and images might be the most important step of all.

"The esthetic reason for delighting in [these] white colonial farmhouses is simple;
white and white alone fully reflects the surrounding lights; white and white alone gives a pure
blue or lavender shadow against the sunlight. At dawn, a white house is pale
turquoise; at high noon it is clear yellow and lavender-blue; in a ripe sunset it is orange
and purple; in short, except on a gray day it is anything but white."

LEWIS MUMFORD

F u n c t i o n

Function changes over time and with each   generation. Proportions may

be absolute, with the size of a window in the same relationship to the size of a door, but

a dining room doesn't have to be used only for meals. An honest appraisal and

understanding of function will go far to guarantee the everyday success of a

space. What matters most is how a room works for you. Function is as much

about ensuring comfort as about having a dishwasher that works efficiently.

"Isn't practicality an aesthetic decision about life?"

ETTORE SOTTSASS

T e x t u r e

A VARIETY OF TEXTURES ANIMATES THE SENSES AND AWAKENS THE SPIRIT. IN THE LIFE OF A ROOM, material and details convey texture: hard and soft, rough and smooth, shiny and matte. Combinations of textures in furnishings and surfaces provide the opportunity for contrast that evokes sensuality: the feel of cool slate and rough sisal on the floor, or crystal prisms dangling from a wrought-iron candelabra. Texture can be altered with the seasons, too. For summer, striped canvas slipcovers and a sisal rug might replace the heavy damask and richly patterned Persian rug that warms a living room in winter. Or texture might be as simple as the look of light muslin hanging softly from wrought-iron curtain rods.

"Style means understanding the importance of combining textures in a room.
And how to do it is something only intuition can tell you."
ANDRÉE PUTMAN

Memory and Wit

MEMORY AND WIT ARE QUALI-TIES THAT PERSONALIZE SPACE. IN A WORLD OF MASS-PRODUCED products and television-defined life-styles, a room designed with a sense of your own signature is crucial. References to personal history and a shared past make a place unique. Humor in the shape of something unexpected always has a welcoming effect.

Collections—the most immediate way to personalize a space—can be made up of many things. They don't have to be antiques and fine art: postcards, mixing bowls, or old-fashioned biscuit tins can be just as interesting. The decorative impulse ranges from a wall stencil that subtly pulls the room together to an oversize piece of art or poster that rivets immediate attention. A well-balanced room should not only function but delight.

"I like houses to be cozy, comfortable, and personal. Not cluttered, but filled with interesting objects and toys and as many jokes as I can get away with."

CANDICE BERGEN

1 Floor : Hardwood
  Area Rug ? Sisal (pr. <u>SIGH-sl</u>)

2 Walls : Stucco, Plaster
  Wallpaper   PICTURES

3 Woodwork
  Paint :

4 Shades ? Blinds   (Venetian)

5 Doors ||||| |||
  hinges, hardware

6 OTHER : moldings, etc.

THE ROOM

Before a single stick of furniture has been moved in, there's the room itself to address. What does it already have going for it? To start, there are three surfaces—floor, ceiling, and walls—that can be treated all alike or each in a different way. Add to that the doors and windows, and all that they suggest, and you've got a room alive with possibilities. Now more than ever is the time to think of textures and materials (hard and soft) and how they relate to needs and pleasures (practical and aesthetic). Furnishings are the style and the personality of a room, while the ceiling, floor, walls, and openings are its structure and true nature. They too contribute to making a room livable.

A WORD ON WOOL

If you can, buy carpets made of wool. It is a natural fiber and performs magnificently. Today, wool carpets are either woven or tufted. Weaving means that the yarn and backing were attached at the same time. In tufted rugs, the wool is punched through and the backing is attached later. Woven rugs are stronger. Rugs made with synthetic materials, especially continuous filament nylon, are a fine, if slightly less durable, alternative to wool.

DAVE LANDY,
ABC Carpet & Home

The floor beneath your feet provides more tactile sensation than any other surface: smooth concrete, cold granite, soft pine. With every step, the foot registers and reacts to the material with which it comes into contact. And yet we tend to ignore uncovered floors. If they are without rugs, we call them bare.

In fact, hard floor materials suggest a vast range of possibilities. Think of the variety of stone, tile, and wood used for flooring and add to that all the possible treatments of those materials. Wood alone can be laid in wide planks with wooden pegs or in narrow strips; in a herringbone pattern; or simply bleached and whitewashed. Stone floors range from rough slate slabs or prefabricated block to highly polished marble squares. There are also ceramic or terra-cotta tiles, as well as stained concrete.

Pattern has recently reemerged as something that can be incorporated into hard flooring. Wood inlays and patterned parquet have a long tradition in American crafts, as does stenciling. Whether it's along the perimeter or covering the center or over the entire surface, stenciling animates a hard floor with elegance and vitality. A square pattern set at a diagonal gives a sense

HOW TO BLEACH A FLOOR

"Mix three parts Bleach A to one part Bleach B and apply to floor. Let 'cure' for three days to bleach. Then thin Japan Color White paint (a shade that artists use) with turpentine to the thickness of wash you want. Use a rag to wipe onto the floor, allowing grain to show through. Repeat process. Then apply two coats of your choice of sealer, sanding between each application. Finish with three coats of flat polyurethane, which dries in one day. The entire procedure takes seven days, and lasts for many years."

SANDRA NUNNERLY, *New York interior designer*

of expanding space to a small room. Besides possessing a visual appeal that brightens a room, bleached and whitewashed floors are easy to maintain and always look fresh.

In general, hard floors tend to be durable, washable, subtle in palette, and evocative of different feelings. An oak floor is warm; a tiled one is cool. Hard floors introduce an element of the natural into the interior world of the man-made.

On the other hand, covered floors are about texture and protection (both of the hard floor and of the feet). Rugs and carpets, be they Persian heirlooms or wall-to-wall, sisal or canvas, offer texture as an experience. When you get up in the morning, your feet are the first part of your body to be exposed to hard reality. They will remember the feeling of soft material underfoot easing the way. There is a visual aspect to floor coverings as well. They provide pattern and color, shape and definition. A patterned rug under the dining table can help to establish boundaries where there are no walls.

Most important, floor coverings offer the advantage of flexibility. They can be moved about according to the occasion, the mood, or the season.

Walls bring out our most primitive insecurities. Too close together, and we feel constricted; too far apart, and we feel lost. But it is not only the placement of walls that trigger so much emotion. Surfaces also convey meaning, and can induce a feeling of comfort or edginess.

There is really no such thing as a plain white wall. Even white comes in a medley of shades. Painted surfaces might be solid or decorated, one color or several. Faux painting can create an illusion of an entirely different world beyond, a clever way to expand on minimal space.

Wallpaper adds pattern, from historic reproductions to the subtlest abstract print. Stucco, paneled wood, and plaster molding speak to tradition. Glass block and metal look contemporary, even avant-garde, depending on the treatment.

Walls could well be an extension of the floor and made of the same concrete, tile, or marble. Like the floor, walls are an opportunity for experimenting with texture. They may be in the background, but the wall's role in animating the life of a room is decidedly up front.

Walls can also move. And as the blanket-on-a-rope climax to that Gable-Colbert classic *It Happened One Night* proved, movable walls can be funny, or at least, as much conversational as convenience pieces. Flexible walls might even make more sense in the home than in the open-plan office. In a room, they can both adorn and serve, providing ornament as well as privacy.

Screens, curtains, and room dividers are about selective transparency. They conceal parts of a room without denying that those other spaces exist. A folding screen—in lacquered wood, painted canvas, upholstered fabrics, or glass and metal—can be sexy, hiding as much as it reveals. Movable walls liberate the imagination, because almost anything that stands can become one: a bookcase turned sideways, a high-backed sofa, or even canvas stretched on a professional dress rack. With so much flexibility, the movable wall ought to be a permanent fixture in the home.

SCREENS AND VISUAL BARRIERS are a flexible way to honor Modernism's comfort-equals-space corollary without sacrificing the just-as-important comforts of intimacy.

By creating partial separations that can divide a room or merely isolate a private corner, a screen or even display- or bookcases provide a division that doesn't diminish the experience of spaciousness.

"A room without books is a body without a soul."
CICERO

VOICE OF WISDOM

Frank Lloyd Wright (1867–1959). Frank Lloyd Wright is by far the most influential architect in the history of modern American design. In his prolific career spanning some sixty-six years, Wright produced more than 600 buildings, many of them private residences.

Wright's philosophy of architecture and home design centered on the notion of simplicity. To Wright, simplicity meant a perfect accord between the beautiful, the practical, and the appropriate. It implied the same integrity and grace, free of the superfluous, that characterizes all things in harmony with nature, from a wildflower to a Japanese print (two favorite examples of Wright's). He called this ideal simplicity of design, organic architecture. And, to this day, organic unity remains one of the most compelling and lasting concepts in architecture.

In Wright's houses, the massive stone or brick hearth (with all its connotations of gathering) served an anchoring role. So, too, did the idea of modern convenience, which Wright conceived of as a minimal amount of exquisitely crafted, built-in furniture of his own design. Above all, Wright believed passionately in the promise of American residential architecture to become the standard by which the whole world would someday live.

ICONS OF INFLUENCE
a wildflower
a stone hearth
a Japanese print
a river rock

"A thing to be simple needs only to

SELECTED SIGNIFICANT BUILDINGS BY FRANK LLOYD WRIGHT

Frederick C. Robie House (1907–9), Chicago; Barnsdall Hollyhock House (1917–20), Los Angeles; Kaufmann House, "Fallingwater" (1935–39), Bear Run, Pennsylvania; Johnson Administration Building (1936–39), Racine, Wisconsin; Solomon R. Guggenheim Museum (1959), New York.

SIMPLICITY

"Simplicity and Repose are qualities that measure
the true value of any work of art. . . . But simplicity is not
in itself an end nor is it a matter of the side of a barn
but rather an entity with a graceful beauty in its integrity
from which discord, and all that is meaningless, has
been eliminated. A wild flower is truly simple."

HOUSES

"There should be as many kinds of houses as there
are kinds (styles) of people and as many differentiations as
there are different individuals. A man who has
individuality (and what man lacks it?) has a right to its
expression in his own environment."

ORGANIC ARCHITECTURE

"Nothing is more difficult to achieve than the integral
simplicity of organic nature amid the tangled
confusions of the innumerable relics of form that
encumber life for us."

be true to itself in organic sense."

Windows. How many windows are there? It's the first question we ask in order to judge how habitable a room might be. The second most important question is, What kind of windows are they? but it is rarely asked. We need windows to thrive physically as well as spiritually. Nothing is simpler, nor more complex. Windows of clear glass, textured glass, colored glass, stained glass. Big bay windows, little round oculi. Interior windows, exterior openings. Windows that frame a view; windows that ventilate. A window might even be a door. Windows should be both aesthetically pleasing and energy-efficient. The relative size of windows can make a room seem larger; depending on their positions, they can activate a breeze. Windows can be picture perfect, or as unexpected as a punch line. A window over the kitchen sink can turn the drab duty of doing the dishes into a meditative moment. Windows are the room's breath of life.

"In describing light, we speak of color, softness, relaxation, memories, excitement, or quietness."

ETTORE SOTTSASS

LOW-E GLASS

The new standard in energy-efficient glass since 1984 is made with a coating that admits direct sunlight, heating up interior furnishings in the winter, but reflects heat away from interiors in the summer. Standard Low-e glass is also known as Northern Low-e; for southern climates, a coating layered with silver that blocks heat has recently been developed.

Windows are also architecture. With the addition of curtains, blinds, and shutters, they can be dressed with fashions that both introduce texture and modulate light. Curtains and shutters are a practical way to deflect light. At the same time, they are all about style and atmosphere. From the sheerest muslin that wafts with every breeze to the most imperial of swags, curtains soften the lines of structure. Wooden blinds strike a more vernacular and architectural note, but blinds made of metal seem very modern. The windows are often the first thing noticed on entering a room. Dressing a window or leaving it bare is as subjective a decision as any concerning furnishings. It affects the entire mood of a room. The patterns of sunlight and shadow cast by window treatments underline the essence of a room's character. People forget the exact upholstery on a chair but always remember the quality of light in a room.

GLASS

Transparent glass allows maximum visibility. Translucent glass is textured on one or both sides and admits about 80% diffused light. Glass block fractures images without entirely blocking out the light.

D o o r s . Although doors rarely provide much of a design bang, they do contribute substance to a room. Exterior doors require more heft than interior ones. But both tend to be standardized when they could be unique. Consider using pocket sliding doors where space is limited, and Dutch doors for light and air or to catch a partial view without inviting intruders. Double doors hint at grandeur; transom doors provide air circulation. Hollow-core and aluminum doors just don't have the weight and solidity of carved oak or patinated steel.

Doors mediate between the public and the private. They can be translucent or transparent, imposing physical, but not always visual, limits. French doors double as windows, bringing light into an interior. Folding doors can act as a wall, transforming one space into two. A wide door says hospitality; a narrow one suggests a secret passage. Behind the door, there is always the promise of discovery.

C e i l i n g . A good ceiling is a prize. The most abbreviated real-estate pitch will always boast if they've got cathedral ceilings, original beams, or ornamental moldings. Ceilings over ten feet high always rate a mention. Ceilings might be an extension of the walls and painted the same color; or an alternating shade to create a heightened sense of expansion or intimacy. Faux paintings and reflective surfaces will draw transfixed attention, while an old-fashioned pressed tin ceiling, like ornamental plastering, bears the stamp of history. Wallpaper on the ceiling may help a child fall asleep; or acoustical tiles could blunt the sound of a teen's favorite music. The ceiling offers the chance for a purely visual gesture, something pleasing to always look up to.

Plastic moldings made of high-density polymers and fiberglass-reinforced plaster are lighter, less expensive, and more fire-retardant than traditional wood moldings. They come prefabricated or can be made to order.

A ceiling that is slightly darker than the walls makes the room appear to expand. Extend the darker shade to the upper 12 to 18 inches of the wall, and add molding to complete the effect.

DOOR DIRECTION

In *Feng Shui: The Chinese Art of Placement,* Sarah Rossbach explains that according to principles of feng shui, the ancient Chinese philosophy of natural design, doors facing northwest promise that your interests will be far-ranging; doors facing toward the northeast guarantee intelligence; toward the southeast, wealth; and toward the southwest, a good spouse.

FURNITURE

If the floors and walls of a room are the strong bones that give it structure, the basic furnishings provide character. Their function is more diverse than merely to provide a place to sit or to eat. Furnishings express value. Every piece of furniture, no matter how modest or refined, conveys information about quality and suitability. Frank Lloyd Wright once said that we should only own what we can appreciate. In furnishings, too, it is your considered choices about living, rather than the expense, that should dictate what furniture to buy and how to use it. In the end, true value resides in choosing pieces that will best serve you as an individual.

QUALITY EQUALS VALUE

"Great design is remarkably straightforward.
Objects of quality seem to escape their own time
limits through a process of judicious, even self-
confident, taking away of that which is not necessary.
The point of the design collection at the
Museum of Modern Art is to show that good design
can be made available to all; expense is
not a criteria. An anonymously made Pyrex
container is about good design as much as
an Alvar Aalto vase."

TERENCE RILEY,
Director of Architecture and Design,
Museum of Modern Art, New York

More than ever before, our lives are shaped by design. From computers to wrapping paper, cars to recycling bins, objects of everyday use are designed. But design is not just a marketing tool; it says something about our increasing awareness and respect for quality. In other words, we understand that good design adds value. Design is not the exclusive right of only those who can afford it. We have learned that good design not only lasts, but it is accessible, too. Such is our definition of a classic. Once, an object owed its status to its rarity, its proportion, its proven appeal, and sometimes its cost. Now we think of classics as also useful, graceful, and appropriate. A No. 2 pencil has its own unique design integrity.

"I firmly believe that plain, simple things are superior to flashy, complicated ones. Something that is simple and satisfying is a greater achievement than something fussy. Good objects are designed with honesty, integrity, simplicity, and guts. A plain glass milk bottle can ultimately be more impressive than an intricate silver gilt pitcher."

TERENCE CONRAN

So does a Louis Vuitton suitcase. Both are made with perfect economy of line, employing durable materials ideally suited to the task.

The economics of investing in classics have also changed. If an important piece of furniture anchors the room, sometimes spending more means spending less overall. However, a pedigree is not always necessary. For those who understand design value, provenance—whether or not a piece is a certifiable original—does not have to be the point. Strong lines, solid materials, and effectiveness are what characterize today's value-rich classics, be they a Corbusier chaise lounge or a Conran's stacking chair.

Chair. In the ergonomics of everyday life, the chair plays a central role. It props you up for breakfast; braces you at a desk; cradles you in comfort at the end of a long day. With each new function, the chair's shape undergoes a dramatic shift in personality. The stiff-backed desk chair and the round-armed reading chair are scarcely related members of the same family. And yet, to understand the most purposeful way to use a chair, it helps to consider the similarities as well as the differences among various chair types.

Unlike most other pieces of furniture, every chair necessarily has a one-on-one relationship to its user. Only one person at a time can claim possession of it. For this reason, the role

LCM DINING CHAIR,
1946, designed by
Charles and Ray Eames

AVERAGE SEAT HEIGHTS
child's chair—8–14"
lounge chair—15 ½"
bench—16 ½"
stacking chair—17"
office swivel posture chair—17¼"
dining or side chair—18"
bar stool—30"

from The American Institute of Architects' Architectural Graphic Standards

that each specific chair fulfills in the life of a room is an open question. Here, personal preference rightly dominates in the choice of chair.

Take the armchair. If all chairs range from hard to soft, purely functional to thoroughly indulgent, the armchair ranks softest. But it is not without purpose: to be successful, the armchair must exude comfort. In its depth, its give, its materiality, and in ways that are perhaps best measured emotionally, the armchair appeals most directly to the individual. After all, in today's crowded and time-pressed lives, a concentrated dose of relaxation—a half-hour spent reading or dozing in an arm-chair—translates into a valuable form of entertainment.

"Today we are sitting in a totally different way than Marie Antoinette sat on a chair or sofa. We are eating in a totally different way than Henry VIII ate. This means that the so-called practical need does not really exist. There are just needs and solutions to needs."

ETTORE SOTTSASS

CHIC SIMPLE CHAIRS THROUGHOUT THE TWENTIETH CENTURY

VIENNA CAFE CHAIR
1859, by Michael Thonet

STARCK CHAIR
1982, by Philippe Starck

ADIRONDACK CHAIR
ca. 1920s, Anonymous

MODEL B33
1930, by Marcel Breuer

TRIPOLINA CHAIR,
ca. 1855, by J. B. Fenby

LOUNGE CHAIR AND OTTOMAN
1956, by Charles Eames

STEEL WIRE "DIAMOND" CHAIR
1952, by Harry Bertoia

TULIP CHAIR
1956, by Eero Saarinen

CROSS CHECK ARMCHAIR
1991, by Frank Gehry

FLEDERMAUS CAFE CHAIR
1905, by Josef Hoffmann

FAMOUS SITTERS

Sphinx of Egypt
Michelangelo's Moses
"Van Gogh's Chair"
Rodin's *Thinker*
Lincoln Memorial
Christine Keeler

"A chair is a very difficult object to design. A skyscraper is almost easier, that is why Chippendale is famous."

LUDWIG MIES VAN DER ROHE

ITALIAN NEOCLASSICAL CHAIR more idiosyncratic than its grander French Napoleonic or its more architectural Biedermeier cousins. Neoclassical designs are now highly sought after because they mix well with most contemporary styles.

LC-2 PETIT CONFORT was designed by Le Corbusier in 1928. Here, tubular steel, so popular with early Modernist designers who had borrowed it from airplane manufacturing, is paired with the softest, down-filled leather cushions. The chair is still in production at Atelier International. Unofficial reproductions are also widely available.

DCW DINING CHAIR in molded plywood by Charles and Ray Eames, 1946, is a fine example of the exuberant post-WWII design spirit. Industrial production values applied to the decorative arts, and organic shapes influenced by scientific discoveries were considered key factors in making affordable chairs for the future. The DCW was manufactured by the Herman Miller Furniture Company and is now a highly collectible twentieth-century antique.

AMERICAN WINDSOR chairs were originally designed in England—the first known example can be traced to Windsor Castle, 1650—but achieved their greatest popularity in early nineteenth-century America. The Windsor chair comes in many variations but usually has a spindled back and is an instantly recognizable archetype. It is still widely produced.

CLEVELAND FIREPROOF ALUMINUM CHAIR is typical of the lightweight office furniture of the Thirties, when aluminum was an exciting new material discovered by the airplane industry. Extremely durable, aluminum chairs are beginning to be collected for their clean lines and brushed finish.

STICKLEY ARMCHAIR was designed in 1905 by Gustav Stickley, who through his works promoted the idea of simple, well-crafted furniture for the masses. This armchair is an adaptation of the English Morris chair, distinguished for its wide, flat arms that offer a convenient ledge for arms, books, or even coffee mugs. Many original designs are available from L. & J. G. Stickley, at auction (for originals), or through other less official sources who have adapted the Mission style.

VOICE OF WISDOM

Elsie de Wolfe (1870–1950). All modern histories of interior decoration must account for Elsie de Wolfe. In fact, she called herself the first interior decorator. True or not, the title has stuck. She was certainly the most flamboyant, and her unique sense of style still carries an impact. At a time when many were beginning to tire of the Gilded Age—its musty Victorian interiors heavy with velvet drapes and crammed with potted palms—Elsie de Wolfe offered Americans fresher interiors. Her love of the light-painted furnishings and airy spaces of eighteenth-century France translated into a modern taste for minimal luxury.

Although her rooms were considered practically barren in comparison to the turn-of-the-century norm, there was nothing retiring about her approach. Indeed, her signature looks—leopard skin on Louis XVI fauteuils, architectural molding set into mirrored plate glass, white-painted furniture against colored walls—managed to convey restraint as well as panache. And she touted common sense, too. Elsie de Wolfe said that a good English chintz was more impressive for being practical than a cheap brocade. And she didn't like "period rooms." To her, they were anathema. Her maxim was to mix it up and make it personal. In a 1982 biography by Jane Smith, Diana Vreeland summed up de Wolfe's contribution when she wrote in the preface, "What Elsie did for decorating in our time will last forever."

ICONS OF INFLUENCE

Louis XIV–XVI
kid gloves
English chintz

"Suitability! Suitab

PRIORITIES

"When I am asked to decorate a new house, my first thought is suitability. My next thought is proportion. Always I keep in mind the importance of simplicity."

COMFORT

"Light, air, and comfort—these things I must always have in a room."

TASTE

"How can we develop taste? Some of us, alas, can never develop it, because we can never let go of shams. We must learn to recognize suitability, simplicity, and proportion, and apply our knowledge to our needs."

BEDROOMS

"I believe that everything in one's house should be comfortable, but one's bedroom must bc more than comfortable: it must be intimate."

lity! Suitability!"

The Coffee Table

Like the pencil Henry Thoreau almost forgot to take to Walden Pond, the coffee table is so much an extension of our daily lives that we've forgotten it's there. It is so smoothly functional, it's invisible. The perfect hub around which to gather furniture and friends, staunch supporter of liquid refreshment for those sprawled on the couch, convenient display space for all manner of objects, the coffee table has never been so much designed as wished into being.

PRECURSORS TO THE COFFEE TABLE

CHINESE K'ANG TABLE
1368–1644. Ceremonial table for the home with the low-to-the-ground proportions adapted by Art Deco furniture.

ITALIAN RENAISSANCE CASSONE
1610–1699. An all-purpose chest for storing objects, especially books.

ENGLISH BUTLER'S TABLE
1710–Present. No well-appointed English governor's mansion lacked one of these tray *cum* tables with folding sides for easy conveyance.

FRENCH BELLE EPOQUE OTTOMAN
1890–1914. A low, cushioned, often round or rectangular piece of support furniture placed close to more formal seating arrangements.

"Oh coffee tables! People are so hung up on them."

MARK HAMPTON

ISAMU NOGUCHI

Originally designed in 1944.
Manufactured by Herman Miller from
1945–72. Reintroduced in 1984.

Dimensions: 50"W; 36"D; 15 3/4"H

Materials: Solid walnut or poplar with
ebony finish; glass.

CLASSIC COFFEE TABLES

SYRIE MAUGHAM

1933. Syrie Maugham's white
lacquered coffee table first appeared
in her living room in *The Studio* magazine
in 1933 and was an instant sensation.

LUDWIG MIES VAN DER ROHE

1937. Barcelona or Tugendhut X-table,
manufactured by Knoll International
40"W; 40"D; 17"H

**CHARLES AND RAY
EAMES**

1951. Laminate-topped ETR,
manufactured by Herman Miller
84"W; 29"D; 10"H

**GENERIC SIXTIES
COFFEE TABLE**

1968. Improvised table, manufactured
at home by placing 3/4" plate glass on
anything (think lobster crate) 16" off floor.

"I pay a fortune for these battered tables, and my husband says, 'Aren't you going to paint them?' And I say, 'You don't understand the concept here.'"

CANDICE BERGEN

Big Tables. If room allows, there should always be one oversize table. Big tables not only lead many lives—inviting guests, supporting objects, offering workspace—but add life. A room will revolve around the biggest table in its midst no matter where it's placed. Chairs gravitate to it, as well as people and activities.

The farmhouse kitchen table remains the favorite. Balanced on four thick legs, it provides strong personality without formal airs. It can take a beating; it improves with wear. Tablecloths need not attend. Large but simple farmhouse tables answer many needs, but the most important one is about gathering.

REMEMBERING BILLY BALDWIN

"On the subject of table heights in a room, Billy always thought that unless you had a pair of tables, the heights should vary so that your eye would not follow the same horizontal line around the room. Of course, if you're using a pair of lamps on either side of a sofa, the tables cannot be different heights."

ARTHUR SMITH, *interior designer*

Occasional Tables arc a relatively new addition to the categories of furniture types. Occasional tables were most likely invented more out of convenience than need. Side tables, coffee tables, stacking tables, and bedside tables all accompany other pieces of furniture as accessories to allow for more comfort, availability, and ease. Slight as they seem—and occasional tables are often scaled-down—they have made themselves essential in our lives, providing display space or even open storage. The right occasional table must fit in two ways: in size proportionate to (although not necessarily matching) the piece it stands besides, and in height to facilitate the purpose it serves. Of course, an occasional table might also stand alone as a still life by the window or its own sculpture of graceful lines.

Why

IN THE AGE OF TELEVISION THE COUCH HAS

a

REPLACED THE DOG AS MAN'S BEST FRIEND.

sofa?

THE GREAT NAPPERS

Alexander the Great , Napoleon, Thomas Edison, Winston Churchill, Harry Truman, Oblomov, Salvador Dali,
Ronald Reagan

BOON COMPANION TO THE TIRED, THE SOFA IS OTHERWISE a designer's nightmare. Its posture is lousy, too slumped or too stiff. Its proportions are ungainly, hogging the focus in a room. Size, not purpose, tends to determine where the sofa must go. Yet the sofa exudes the essence of comfort. Even straight-backed versions, descendants of those backless chaises featured at Roman symposia, are meant to enhance conversational ease. Above all, the sofa is an invitation to nap, cushioned enough to cosset limbs, but not so flat or wide as to imitate a bed. For a bed implies taking the business of sleeping seriously, while an armchair rarely allows full neck extension. For many, the sofa is the only legitimate place for a nap. It alone serenely conveys the serious napper to the half-dream, half-conscious state that is the true gift of the great sofa.

Z

The Surrealist painter Salvador Dalí took his naps with a built-in alarm, sitting up in a chair with a spoon in his hand and a tin plate between his feet. Dalí's nap was over when the spoon dropped into the plate.

Z

A fifteen-minute afternoon nap is deep enough to allow the body a sufficient amount of slow-wave sleep to fuel seven hours of activity.

Z

A.M.

M.

Beds are a short pause be

P.M.

Beds. Newly independent, just married, or just moving in, all people at some point in life need to choose the bed they will lie in. But what really is a bed? A futon on the floor, a metal frame on castors, a padded headboard, a trundle, or a canopy—the options are too many to make a quick decision easy. Today, beds are bigger than ever. Several historic

ween waking states.

styles have recently reemerged, namely the sleigh bed and the four-poster. The padded headboard—ideal for reading in bed—is detachable and can be temporarily removed, or replaced altogether with a big pile of pillows. The fundamental decision to make about beds is to figure out if you want to sit upright and therefore need back support or sink softly, perhaps, into down.

SHOPPING FOR A MATTRESS? Be sure to ask: how many coils? (300–450 in a full- to king-size bed is the best range); how big are the springs? (6- to 12-inch springs give a desirable bounce); what's the thickness of the steel in the coils? (#12½ to #14 gauge wire is recommended. The lower the number, the more durable; higher numbers make softer beds); how many turns in each spring? (the more turns, the more bounce. The range is 6 to 8 turns).

Above all, get a good box spring made with springs instead of a wood-frame foundation with foam, unless you want a very hard bed. If you opt for foam, make sure it has a minimum density of 2.0 lbs per cubic foot.

CHARLES BECKLEY,
custom bed maker

The coil-spring mattress was invented in 1860.
Ancient Egyptians were buried in their beds.
Ancient Romans slept in their underwear.

THREAD COUNT
indicates the number of threads per square inch in a cotton sheet; the higher the number the stronger and softer the fabric. The thread count of sheets ranges between 150 and 350.

CALIFORNIA KING SIZE
sheets (72" x 84") are shorter but wider than standard King size sheets (76" x 80").

IT'S IN THE FILLING
"Down and feathers" on the label of a quilt or duvet indicates more down than feathers. "Feathers and down" means the opposite. The more down a quilt contains, the warmer it will be.

THE BIGGEST BED IN HISTORY
measured 18 feet wide and 12 feet long. It was a gift from Philip the Good to Isabella of Portugal in the fifteenth century.

Built-in Storage.

Ever more limited space is part of the modern condition. And storage is the unglamorous design problem that comes with it. Storage puts high demands on our most dubiously developed faculties—for organization and logic. Whether it's a matter of deep-sixing your tenaciously preserved high-school yearbooks or establishing a ready-to-go shelf for exercise equipment, storage calls for many degrees of access and size. In addition to all the traditional objects needing storage—clothes, blankets, and toys, for instance—new technology has

ORGANIZATION
The instinct to organize has gone public with a host of stores and companies now at your service to provide everything from instant shoe racks to complete custom-designed closets. Start by storing these numbers:

Hold Everything (national stores and mail-order storage products) 800 421 2264

California Closet Company (nationally franchised custom laminate storage consultants) 415 433 9999

Closet Systems Corporation (custom closet designers) 800 400 1401

Organization U.S.A. (mail-order modular storage systems) 800 366 ELFA

introduced at least one entirely new class of objects to store: media equipment, including stereo, CD player, VCR. For the very lucky few, there may be space enough simply to stash such equipment out of sight and mind in a specially designated room. The rest of us must be more imaginative. One way to organize storage is to divide it into two categories: built-in versus movable. The Shakers perfected the design of the built-in wall of drawers, each appropriately sized to fit its contents. It's an idea that looks better than ever today. Built-in storage can be anything from a walk-in closet to a wooden draining rack for dishes.

Movable Storage.

History offers a brilliant solution for expanding storage space: movable containers. In the Middle Ages, all-purpose chests held entire households on the move and then doubled as tables and beds on arrival. In the early nineteenth century, Napoleon established the fashion for portable campaign furniture. Our own lives are not so lightweight; and yet, we could certainly adapt the notion of movable storage. Armoires, distinguished period pieces for rooms without closets and traditionally used for linens and clothes, might be adapted to contain your media equipment. Trunks and chests could do double duty, utilizing both the inside and the top. The very notion of visible storage could be exploited more, with bookcases, tables, and shelves combining the services of both display and storage. A thick picture railing attached to the wall can provide enough rim to lean pictures. Built-in closets were not invented until the early nineteenth century, and yet we have already forgotten the multitude of ways in which people once stored their possessions. Most important, movable storage in the home lends itself to more flexible ways of using space.

CEDAR SCENTS

Mothballs work by poisoning with formaldehyde. Cedar linings for closets, chests, and drawers preserve clothing by deterring moths from laying eggs. Cedar smells better, too. A sprig of dried rosemary also repels moths and at the same time adds a pleasant fragrance.

I n d i r e c t lighting generates purely emotional responses from people. If a space is romantic and cozy or, obversely, clinical and depressing, it's because of the background lighting. Lighting analysts claim that feelings of relaxation and privacy are encouraged by nonuniform, peripheral lighting, while bright, uniform lights suggest clarity and spaciousness. The trick of indirect lighting is to illumine without merely focusing on one specific object. Background lighting brings out the character of a space.

Indirect lighting actually works through diffusion, reflection, and bouncing off surfaces. There are many styles and types of indirect lights: torchères, sconces, floor lamps, wall fixtures, recessed lights and pendules, even task lights (such as Richard Sapper's classic Tizio lamp) turned upward to reflect off the ceiling. Indirect lighting can make a small room appear larger, especially when the walls are light and reflective rather than dark and light-absorbing. Overall, the oblique function of indirect lighting is every bit as elemental to the success of a room as the most pointed task light.

"More Light!"

GOETHE'S LAST WORDS

WALL WASHERS are angled-down lights that illuminate a wall of paintings, prints, or bookcases. Place fixtures no more than 18" from the wall, and use tungsten reflector bulbs.

D i r e c t lighting is focused on getting something done. Installing the right lighting system calls for taking an inventory of activities and the kind of lighting that will enhance, not hinder, them.

In considering the options for direct lighting, one must think about glare, reflectivity, and position. Task lights should always be movable. The rule of thumb is that the shade should be set at about eye level for maximum effect. Halogen lights, and now energy-efficient compact fluorescents, are particularly well-suited for direct lighting because they do not throw off much heat. In direct lighting, the tint or color that the light casts is not so crucial, but protecting the eyes from glare without creating excessive shadows is. For more general tasks, say in the kitchen, a diffuser over the direct light might be desirable. Integrating technology and aesthetics is the aim of good direct lighting.

CANDLESTICK LAMP

COLONIAL SCONCE

THE TABLE LAMP

HIGH TECH TASK

NOGUCHI TABLE LAMP

ARTS AND CRAFTS DESK LAMP

HURRICANE GLASS AND CAND

ALUMINUM MODERNE

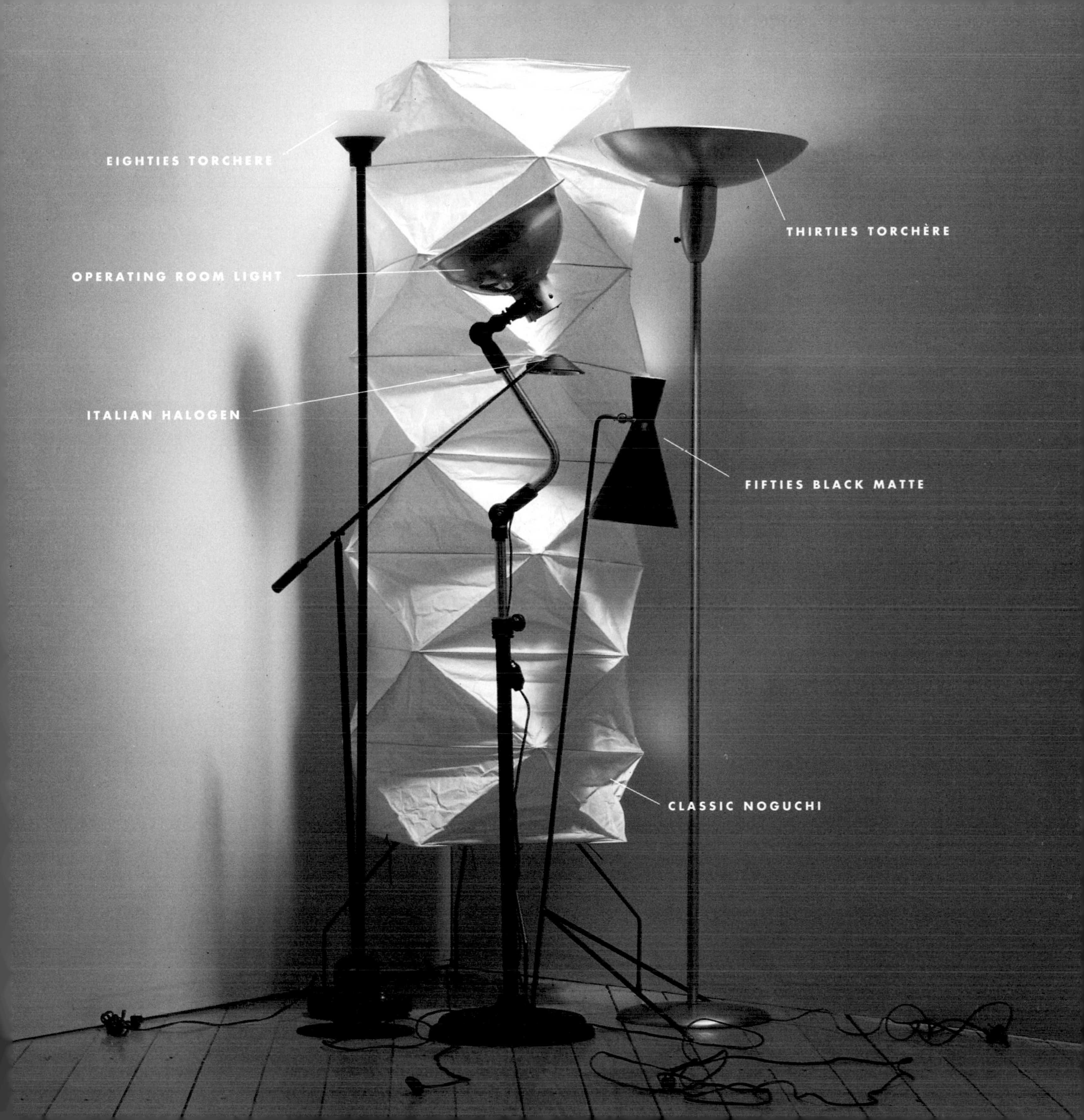

EIGHTIES TORCHERE

OPERATING ROOM LIGHT

ITALIAN HALOGEN

THIRTIES TORCHÈRE

FIFTIES BLACK MATTE

CLASSIC NOGUCHI

LIVING

"Living well is the best revenge."

GEORGE HERBERT,

British poet and clergyman, 1593–1633

"Violet and Joe have arranged their furnishings in a way that might not remind anybody of the rooms in *Modern Homemaking* but it suits the habits of the body. . . . Everything is put where a person would like to have it, or would use or need it. So the dining room doesn't have a dining table with funeral-parlor chairs. It has big deep-down chairs and a card table by the window covered with jade, dracena, and doctor plants until they want to have card games or play tonk between themselves."

TONI MORRISON,

Jazz

Do you have a dining room you hardly use? Is the bedroom an unofficial cineplex? In the past, each room was dedicated to one specific function. There was a sitting room for family gatherings, a parlor in which to entertain, a breakfast room, and perhaps even a smoking room. Service areas were kept strictly from view. After W.W. II, the barriers between rooms began to dissolve. The new open-plan living room had zones, instead of walls, to separate eating and entertaining. In the Seventies, adventuresome people moved into industrial lofts in former warehouses with no definition at all. Today, the point isn't so much about tearing down walls as it is about accommodating the wide variety of ways in which individuals occupy space. It's important to ask, How do I really live? If the bedroom doubles as your home office, or the kitchen is the place where entertaining is liveliest, don't fight it. Let the design serve both ends. And above all, make room for a private refuge. Designing spaces that are not only flexible but multipurpose is the surest way to maximize your pleasure in using them.

"It seems incongruous that the bedroom in the house, is a

S l e e p   s p a c e .   The bedroom is a sanctuary. It is where we sleep and where we dream. And yet it doesn't need to be the exclusive domain of passive activity. Many people prefer working in bed to sitting at a desk. Today, anyone whose sleep space doubles as a home office should also consider installing flexible lighting—bright, direct light (natural, if possible) for the daytime, and indirect, soft lighting for evenings.

Then there are those who treat the bedroom as

om, which is by far the most personal
so the most neglected." TERENCE CONRAN

an entertainment center for family and friends. Along with the living or recreation room, the bedroom is the most likely area to be used as a media room. That might call for installing specific cabinets to hold media equipment. Finally, space for a bed does not necessarily require a room all its own. For anyone who thinks of the bedroom strictly in terms of sleeping, there are other options. A Murphy bed, sleeper sofa, bed alcove, or daybed may be all that's required. The space is then free to be used more effectively.

Evelyn Waugh: "We shared what had once been a dressing-room and had been changed to a bathroom twenty years back by the substitution for the bed of a deep, copper, mahogany-framed bath that was filled by pulling a brass lever heavy as a piece of marine engineering; the rest of the room remained unchanged; a coal fire always burned there in the winter. I often think of that bathroom—the water colors dimmed by steam and the huge towel warming on the back of the chintz armchair—and contrast it with the uniform, clinical, little chambers glittering with chromium-plate and looking-glass, which pass for luxury in the modern world."

from Brideshead Revisited

The bathroom. No room in the house has undergone more of a transformation in recent years than the space in which we bathe. No longer limited to the purely hygienic, it is getting larger and more pleasure-conscious. Thanks to its usually removed location, it makes an ideal refuge. It might even be furnished as a sitting room. Whether changes are as simple as adding a chair, bookshelf, and some plants or a more radical renovation depends on how much time you spend there. The addition of a skylight or, if practical, large windows, or even French doors to a private patio breaks down further the notion that bathrooms have to be small, inhibited water closets. Putting in exercise equipment makes sense too, when you think of this room as an all-around place for indulging your sense of personal well-being.

As in any non-traditional floor plan, transforming bath space into a private refuge is a decision that may mean subtracting square footage from another room, most likely a bedroom or adjoining closet. Accommodating desires while accepting trade-offs is the only way to realize personalized living patterns.

The kitchen is the room with the most protean personality. It can be as small as a narrow galley or it can stretch to embrace the entire family clan. Increasingly, this is where entertaining takes place. People often associate pleasure and generosity with the rituals of preparing food. The traditional farmhouse kitchen with its oversize heavy, wooden table captures the essence of that bountiful feeling. It hardly matters whether you live in the country or the city. This is cooking space as social hub. The kitchen-entertainment center is another possibility. In this case the kitchen has a television, VCR, and CD player. Furnished with an armchair or sofa, the kitchen is a cozy place to read. The kitchen can also be command central for work, with phone, fax, and Rolodex. Then there are those who eat out instead. For them, a narrow kitchen with shipshape efficiency may be the most practical. An undercounter refrigerator, a stovetop without ovens, and a shelf-installed microwave are the minimum features to expect in a compact kitchen.

COUNTER EVOLUTION. "In rethinking the philosophy of the kitchen, I realized the need for a new approach to counter spaces in terms of height and materials. First, there should be a stainless steel or granite cooktop that is impervious to food acids and can handle very hot pans; then, two different heights for food preparation and chopping, [made] both of hard end- or flat-grain wood, such as maple, cherry, or oak. A water-repellent teak or stainless steel surface that slopes surrounds the sink. The sink itself should be at the highest level to make working in the basin (generally 8 to 10 inches deeper) comfortable. The chopping block is then about two inches lower. Finally, think about installing another counter six inches below that—or slightly higher than a table—for small appliances such as a Cuisinart, juicer, and coffeemaker that can also double as a food prep area for children."

JOHNNY GREY, *custom kitchen designer*

"The beauty of a spoon is breathtaking."

ANDRÉE PUTMAN

D i n i n g   S p a c e . Victim of contemporary mores that favor informality over protocol, the dining room today is often left empty—a reminder of the days when families conducted themselves more officially. Few people have room to spare for a silent monument.

The dining room needs to be reinvented. At the center of the room, the dining table points the way to a more active life. Massive and sturdy, wide and long, it suggests many more practical uses than the serving of dinner. There's plenty of space for spreading out homework, tossing the

"The dining room isn't going to be around mucl
like a studio for sketching, working, eating, and conversa
a drawer for penc

daily mail, or signing monthly bills. In one corner there might be a stack of books you want to remember to read; the other side is lush with overgrown plants but still leaves room for a few place settings. Perhaps a radio might come in handy to entertain the solitary diner. With the dining table in constant use, the room itself becomes a magnet for people. A table crowded with objects is more inviting, enticing passersby to sit down and chat, or simply browse. And, of course, there will be times for inviting guests to enjoy a meal.

onger. It isn't used enough. Mine is already more

on. My dining room table is more like a desk. It even has

s and for napkins."

GEOFFREY BEENE

DETAILS

PERSONALIZING
Next to painting
a room, changing
the hardware is
probably the quickest
and most effective
way to give a space
its own distinctive
personality.

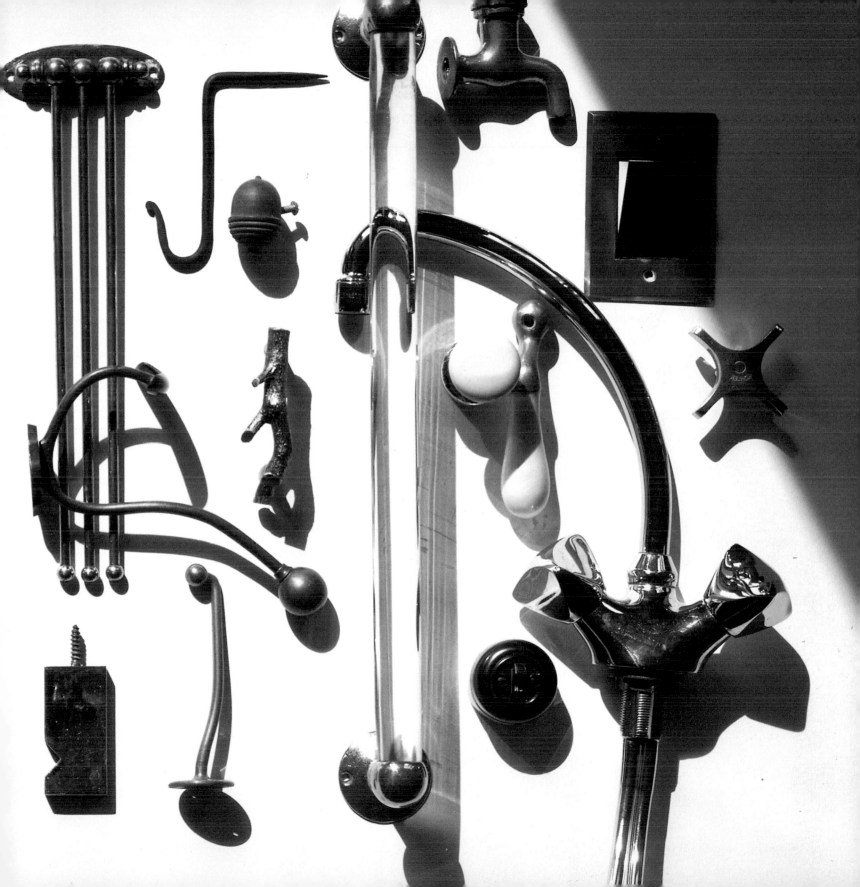

VOICE OF WISDOM

Andrée Putman intuits style with every glance; and her international reputation as design's most suave tastemaker is undisputed. In the tradition of such great interior designers as Elsie de Wolfe and Syrie Maugham, this native Parisian was not professionally trained, developing her expertise over twenty years of design work "just for friends." Earlier stints at French magazines and in marketing established beyond doubt Putman's "eye" and business savvy. Her attention to detail is legendary. Nothing is too minor to be designed, says Putman, who has designed everything from tableware to car interiors, pencils to hotels. In 1978, Putman founded Écart International to reintroduce overlooked classics of early Modernist design by Eileen Grey (see rug, right), Robert Mallet-Stevens, and Mariano Fortuny, among others. She has also created boutiques for the major lights of the fashion world as well as offices for the dynamic French Minister of Culture Jack Lang. In America, her design of the interior of Morgans in New York City set a new standard of sleek, elegant, and minimalist luxury in hotel style. Putman has an unmistakable signature look: monochromatic colors, striking juxtapositions, sculptural furniture, serenity. She once displayed a precious Swiss watch on a pillow of horsehair, and used layered mosquito netting for window shades. As design critic Martin Filler once put it, Andrée Putman is "a minimalist who never denies the senses."

ICONS OF INFLUENCE

a spoon
wooden bowls
apothecary jars
Thonet chairs

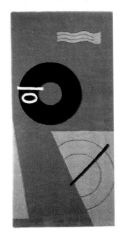

"Style is to see beauty

SELECTED WORKS

Morgans Hotel (1984), New York; Palladium Night Club, with Arata Isozaki (1984), New York; Museum of Contemporary Art conversion (1984), Bordeaux, France; Office interiors for Jack Lang, Minister of Culture (1985), Paris, France; Saint James Club Hotel (1987), Paris, France.

AUTHENTIC STYLE

"Unless you have a feeling for that secret knowledge that modest things can be more beautiful than anything expensive, you will never have style."

COMFORT

"Of course, I love seven pillows behind me, but physical comfort is never the first thing. I prefer spiritual comfort, by which I mean space, light (natural, as well as artificial), contrast of textures, and pure lines. I never look for literal comfort, but for something that allows my mind to rest."

COLOR

"I love colors when they don't exist too much. Life always comes with its own color: your friends, flowers, things. So you don't have to have so much of it in your decor."

n modest things."

Detail is about emotional comfort and sensory richness. A room can be furnished from top to bottom; but without the proper details it will never truly look finished. Similarly, an apparently empty room may on second look reveal itself to be deeply luxurious if its constructed elements are beautifully crafted. Detailing can be structural, historic, massive, or minimal. It can be part of the overall design scheme, or a purely personal gesture. Architectural moldings and baseboards can unify the disparate elements in a room with several zones, or even hide uneven construction. Interesting hardware—a glass doorknob or figurative cabinet pull—can add a custom-made feeling to a flimsy door or unremarkable stock cabinet. Such details endow space with the character that people—no longer satisfied living in bare boxes—crave. The recent boom in salvaging architectural artifacts for home decor proves it. Whether the finishing touches are period-inspired or strictly personal, details add style.

Frame the view, if curtains are not your style. When ungarnished windows look bare, try trimming with strips of architectural molding to add instant distinction.

Fabrics bring a sense of fashion's versatility to a room; they can be changed easily with each season or with a mood. There are two ways to approach fabrics in a room: introducing them through the surroundings, such as floor coverings, window treatments, or fabric on the walls, or else through upholstered and slip-covered furniture. Using ornamental textiles as accents is an excellent way to disguise a room that otherwise lacks architectural interest. Pillows covered in vibrant fabrics can look like jewels against the background of a solid-colored chair. In the Middle Ages, castle dwellers discovered how thick textiles could muffle echoes and cut drafts. Out of their experience came the art of tapestry weaving. Fabrics can compensate a dark room with their own brilliance. Remember, too, that the tactile interest that comes with adding fabrics and textiles to a room provokes a sensual response that goes well beyond the merely visual.

HOW TO PUT ON A SLIP COVER

"First, there are three different pieces with zippers: body, back, and seat. Put each one on ever so damp, never bone dry. I like the baggy look, but leaving covers in the dryer will make them too wrinkly. Slip on over the body using the arms to line it up. Make sure the slip has some extra fabric to tuck in—that's for the look, and to keep the fabric from twisting out of place. Then, give each cushion the good old bounce around: that should do it."

RACHEL ASHWELL, *founder of Shabby Chic*

Defining objects fulfill our need for context. Surrounding ourselves with the things we love is a response to far more than the dictates of structure or design. No matter where we are, we need to create a sense of place to be comfortable. Be it simple or ornate, a room is ours only as long as it's inhabited with our things. A hotel suite is never quite comfortable until half the contents of the suitcase are strewn about. The so-called function of objects is often to define an image of self, preserve memories, or tell a story. In a home, the small objects we choose to bring together don't need to be extraordinary if they have wit, personality, and an interesting shape. Inspired collectors often rely on their instincts in selecting artworks more than on the facts of an object's origins. And there is something of the collector in anyone who is careful in choosing decorative things. Objects express not only preference, but humor, history, sensuality, and memory. They reflect the soul of a room's inhabitants.

The secret of good display is to go to the extreme. Miscellaneous objects placed on a table or shelf tend to disappear. Try grouping together objects that are all of one color or material. Or, set one piece with an interesting shape in splendid, sculptural isolation.

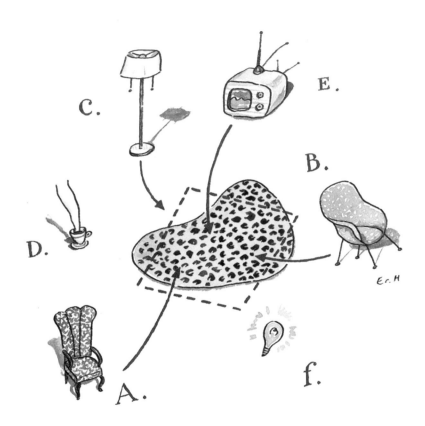

C.

E.

B.

D.

A.

f.

Er. H

MIXING

"I have no recipe for how to combine things. But you must be sincere. And if you are, strangely, it will succeed."

ANDRÉE PUTMAN

People fret so much about "What goes with what" without ever realizing that the easiest way to get it right is to please yourself. The truth is that we all too often try to figure out what a room should look like according to fashion's dictates rather than our own. When putting together a room, it's much better to start by understanding a few principles of composition. Then follow your truest instincts in bringing together the pieces that suit your activities best. First, balance is important. Never let one value outweigh all the others. Whether it's a color, a size, or a pattern, play one against the other. To something dark, add a flash of light; to something massive, something sculptural; to the serious, something witty. If you follow your own preferences, it will help you to maintain a consistent framework in a room. If you like something, chances are it will "go" with the other things you've chosen. That's the real key to mixing, not matching.

HIGH-TECH AND TRADITION.

THE LARGEST PIECE OF FURNITURE IN A ROOM NOT ONLY SETS THE TONE BUT IS A POINT OF DEPARTURE.

Here, it's a sleigh bed from the Thirties that has some Deco characteristics, such as clean, simple lines and a veneer made from an exotic wood (Madagascar mahogany). Otherwise, in terms of shape, this is a rather traditional piece of furniture. Beside its large mass, a metal garden table with spidery legs stands in contrast. A contemporary Tizio lamp—an icon of High-Tech design at its best if ever there was one—juxtaposes its own angularity against the curves of bed and screen, showing how High-Tech and tradition can work together in unexpected ways. Texture abounds, although it's subtle, as in the table's brown rust, the bed's deep polish, and, especially, the screen's oyster silk damask with cast-iron tacks. The patterning on both the screen and the worn dhurrie rug steer the overall tableau away from turning overly monochromatic.

EMPIRE AND VICTORIAN.

IN THE RIGHT CONTEXT, ECCENTRICITY IS ALWAYS
WELCOME. AND SURELY NOTHING SAYS "QUIRKY" FASTER
than this Victorian "Gothic" wooden chair. Notice its whirligig swirls,
miniature rosettes, and pointed-arch back, all painted white. It not only rivets
attention; it needs a steady background. A wide plane of canvas calms without
disappearing. Indeed, the screen is a brilliant instance of adaptive reuse. Canvas
is stretched over a one-time commercial dress rack and attached with clothes-
lines. The addition of a rug with a very bold pattern of its own takes daring,
but it works. Why? Because the rug's lines are geometric, not curvy; magnified,
not miniaturized. Opposites, as always, attract. But within the contrast, there's
consistency between the color of the chair's seat pillow and the rug's red
stripe. The gilt frame of an American Empire-style mirror reflects the
same shape of the screen on a smaller scale and in richer gold hues. A simple
side table—not a period piece, no particular patina—completes the picture.

FIFTIES AND MISSION.

THIS ROOM SETTING, IN SPITE OF USING MOSTLY PERIOD PIECES (BOTH AUTHENTIC AND IMITATION), DOESN'T LOOK dated. It's all in the juxtapositions. Grouped with nothing but their own kind, any one of them might appear too historic. Mixed, the room looks strikingly contemporary. The desk, from the Fifties, is suspended on the skinniest possible steel supports. Its black-lacquered surfaces gives it an added fillip of sophistication. A Noguchi floor lamp and faux Biedermeier side chair (constructed from painted sheet metal) make good company, possessing the same thick/thin dimensions. In fact, by exaggerating the contrast between its oversize shade and slight stick body, the lamp transforms furniture to sculpture. The Arts & Crafts oak chair designed at the turn of the century by Harvey Ellis has more weight than the other pieces, but its linear shape and even-toned oak finish make it not only compatible but fascinating as the desk's partner. Solid flooring in black or white might have made the room look too slick, while the chevron design of this Fifties rug makes a graphic gesture big enough to embrace all.

TRIBAL AND DECO.

MIXING IS ABOUT MORE THAN STYLE SWAPPING. ROOMS OUGHT TO PROVIDE A RANGE OF EXPERIENCES AS WELL.

The big leather armchair, designed in 1988 by Dakota Jackson, embodies the spirit of both glamour and comfort. It's supple, svelte, deep, and reminiscent of Art Deco. Due to the chair's generous bulk, any table close by should be low and easy. It's always a good idea to counteract scales so that no one size can dominate the room. Recycling an African wash bench into a coffee table is not so farfetched as it sounds once you notice the similar proportions of the chair's arms and the wooden bench's legs.

Screen and rug gain strength from their similarities as well as their differences. They share an earthy brown-black palette with a regular pattern. Only the rug's design is small-scale and geometric, while the mysterious circles on the screen are drawn broadly on canvas that has been treated to look like tooled leather. Here, rich combinations are seductive both to the eye and to the touch.

WELL-CRAFTED AND WITTY.

WHEN PEOPLE TALK ABOUT GOOD LINES, THEY USUALLY MEAN A CLASSIC SEVERITY, AS IN THE strong jaw and cheek of a model or the columns of an ancient Greek temple. But in a room, good lines suggest a varied blend of curving and straight, sensuous and simple. In this tableau, the cursive script on a rug by Christine Vanderhurd is a witty way to add good lines. On top of it, a straight-legged table is made of a dark metal, lending a contemporary edge without cutting too deep. The rug's humorous bent is then picked up by the zigzag hem of a slipcover for a nondescript side chair. Today's creative slips are a great way to throw tradition a curve and, while you're at it, reinvent the personality of a chair. A four-tiered copper lamp on the table is an unusual example of an American Arts & Crafts piece. The splay-legged stool is a well-known American Windsor form that suddenly looks more interesting in such mixed company. And that's the point.

SMART HOUSE

"They walked down the hall of their soundproofed Happylife Home, which had cost them thirty thousand dollars installed, this house which clothed and fed and rocked them to sleep and played and sang and was good to them. Their approach sensitized a switch somewhere and the nursery light flicked on when they came within ten feet of it."

RAY BRADBURY, *"The veldt," 1950*

"When I wrote 'The veldt' and 'There Will Come Soft Rains' more than forty years ago, the technology behind the stories was in its babyhood and the smart houses I described would have cost a fortune. Now you can replicate something very close to them for $20,000. Yesterday's fantasy has become today's affordable reality. People might go on about the negative impact of technology, but today the output of all the film studios of Hollywood, the sounds from the finest concert halls in the world, the knowledge and the glory of the greatest libraries—the riches of both the ancient and modern worlds—are at our fingertips in our own homes."

RAY BRADBURY

Personal and home technologies are one of the fastest-growing markets in electronics. Already the House of Tomorrow looks like a relic of yesteryear. Not so long ago, self-starting coffee makers sounded futuristic; now there are houses that talk. The so-called Smart House capable of telling each room to play certain music when the lights are low, contact a service operator to solve a malfunction, or draw a bath of exactly 98 degrees to be ready for you when you get home will soon be under construction at a housing development near you. In planning your own Smart House you should be aware that home technologies are all headed in the direction of integration as well as digitization. Understanding what's in store ten years from now will enable you to take advantage of what's already available today.

S M A R T

THE FIRST KEY TO THE TOTAL HOME IS COMMUNICATION AMONG

APPLIANCES, POWER SOURCES, COMPUTERS, TELEPHONE, HEATING

and air-conditioning (hvac), audio-video equipment, and the outside world. Some of the options for replacing

conventional wiring include bundled cables, low-frequency radio waves, and infrared signals. Once a

communications network is established, it will be possible to assign any light to any switch, and to provide heat,

light, music to any area or room according to any mode (or mood). With appliances programmed to take

advantage of low or off-hour rates, savings in terms of both energy and cost will be considerable. The hvac system of the future is loaded with energy-conserving apparatuses (built-in humidifiers, air purifiers, energy-recovery ventilators, carbon-monoxide monitors), enabling each house to recycle its own air. Heat-based dishwashers, clothes dryers, and other appliances are already available, using microwaves to do the job instantaneously with no loss of energy. Smart windows reflect or absorb light and heat depending on the temperature. They can even switch from clear to opaque according to your needs. In terms of security, linked communications are ever

H O U S E

more essential. Auto-dialing outside numbers (from the police station to your parents) is already part of the standard equipment. Next it will be possible to install voice- or motion-activated video monitors that can send images to any television in the house. Remote-control power locks—adapted from technology now in place on many cars—will soon be on every door and window. Another safety feature possible once power sources throughout the house are linked will be the "dumb outlet" that only charges when it senses a load.

TERMS

In the household of the future, these are words you'll need to know:

HIGH DEFINITION TELEVISION (HDTV) offers theater-quality resolution, digital sound, and wide-screen viewing. Standards must first be established by the FCC before reaching the consumer.

MICROCHIP

The size of a quarter but with the power to monitor the entire house, the microprocessor is the "engine" that drives electronic products. Processor chips are already revolutionizing the integration and coordination of home appliances.

How to install a house-wide power network is the work of professionals. The average home owner wants to know only that the Smart House will be simple to operate. And the universal remote-control set with its own microprocessor (PCs in miniature, but also known as the cordless mouse or magic wand) is supposed to be the solution. Sized to fit the hand, the universal remote should be as easy (or as difficult) to work as today's television remote controls. Even better, the next wave in technology—voice-activated electronics—will allow people to issue spoken commands without ever having to learn how to manipulate a keypad.

In a Smart House, "diagnostic chips" embedded in an appliance will be able to call service operators and have them analyze and even fix malfunctions over the phone. While all of these technologies could be available in every newly constructed home, to retrofit existing houses and establish standards are issues still to be resolved before the Smart House can become our house.

WORKING AT HOME IS NO LONGER CHILD'S PLAY NOW THAT MORE THAN 30 MILLION Americans work where they live. The numbers suggest a vast migration from traditional office situations to home

PERSONAL DIGITAL ASSISTANT (PDA) takes personal computers in a new direction. The PDA will be able to send faxes; receive and send messages; even tell you how to get to the Louvre if you're lost in Paris.

garage. For all that, it has to be professional. The home office, in fact, demands an extremely high degree of technological proficiency to handle operations that a support staff might deal with in a more traditional office. Quick to follow trends,

H O M E O F F I C E.

settings that are more flexible, if also more spatially constrained. For most, the luxury of having a work space that's completely separate from the rest of the house is not often practicable. The home office is more likely jerry-rigged someplace between the guest bedroom, the hall, a maid's room, and the

DOLBY SURROUND SOUND is a coding technology that adds digital-quality sound to audio systems for an effect of totally enveloping sound. It uses four speakers.

LASERDISC The ultimate (so far) in home movies, the laserdisc holds both video and audio information played back on a laserdisc player via reflected laser beams.

most manufacturers have issued computer, printing, photocopy, and fax machines scaled down for home-office use. In considering these machines, the important question to ask yourself is about the volume of work required, since most home-office equipment does not carry the power of larger machines.

For the standard home office, the essential pieces of equipment are the phone, fax, personal computer, printer, and some well-chosen furniture. Recycling an old dining chair for the desk works only for a while—furniture that's meant to be used for work will not only preserve your health but increase your productivity. Well aware of the booming business in home offices, telephone companies are beginning to supply the home office with an ever wider range of services, including dial-by-voice and even assigning particular rings so you can distinguish your mother's call from your employer's.

Though not yet perfected in terms of readable image, video-phones are already on the market. When it comes to modems and copy machines, spatial requirements expand exponentially. Built-in drawers, armoires, and closets are a few at-home storage alternatives. Closets should be deep enough for file cabinets.

In personal computers, new technologies will focus on specific and interactive tasks. PCs that allow writing directly on the screen or that understand spoken commands arc innovations expected to become the new standard someday.

HOME ENTERTAINMENT.

IN NO OTHER AREA OF HOME LIFE ARE PEOPLE MORE WILLING TO

EXPERIMENT AND TO SPEND THAN ON HOME ENTERTAINMENT.

The demand for ever higher definition in televisions and for cleaner sound in audio systems constantly

advances technology. At home, the goal is consolidation, simplification, and whole-house distribution.

The first step is the telecomputer that combines personal computers and high-resolution televisions to make audio,

video, graphic, and textural information available simultaneously. While the telecomputer is all about interaction,

CD-ROM (Compact Disc-Read Only Memory) represents the beginning of a vast network of reference-only programs that will spur an educational revolution. With CD-ROM, you can not only call up information on the life and times of Beethoven but also hear a sampling of his music, and then try to match it to similar compositions from any other period.

Electronics will alter how we decorate our homes, too, once digitally produced artworks (or your choice of any image) start appearing on wall screens throughout the house.

Virtual reality, originally a science fiction conceit, is already in use as an aid to the prospective home builder who would like to

UNIVERSAL REMOTE
Likely to be the most popular "gadget" of the future, Universal Remote consolidates all controls. It operates on signals sent either by radio frequency or infrared rays, so that aiming the "zapper" will not be necessary.

COMPACT DISC-READ ONLY MEMORY (CD-ROM)
is a compact disc that can store sound, photographs, movies, and text. Kodak has recently issued Photo-CDs for storing photographs that you can play back on a television or computer screen.

MULTIMEDIA
It does not mean marketing blitz. Rather, it stands for multiple ways of retrieving information— through image, text, photo, movie—and making connections that draw from all segments.

"walk" through a floor plan before building the house. With the help of a computer-loaded visor and "data gloves," virtual reality tries to duplicate the sensations of any record-able experience. Once it has been absorbed by the entertainment industry through movies and promotions, expect it to come home. As always with new technologies, some will become a part of our lives, while others reach a quick dead end. Most Smart House technologies are designed to be upgraded. The opposite is often true for home entertain-ment, where planned obsolescence is part of the marketing strategy. The only sure way to be current is to stick with what works for you.

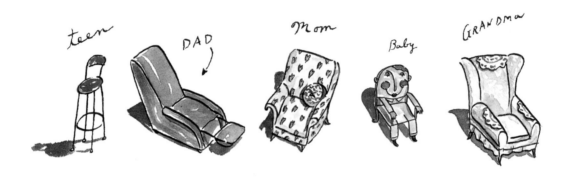

GENERATIONS

The definition of the family continues to expand, reaching beyond immediate relatives to enrich everyone's experience. The extended family provides invaluable learning opportunities as well as reinforcing the values of community. This chapter addresses design as it applies to different age groups, from toddler to teen to senior citizen. These are select phases in a full life-cycle, each of which needs to be acknowledged with celebration and respect. At every stage, empowerment is the goal of design. How do you enable an individual at any age to maintain a sense of control over the home environment? The answer is to provide the appropriate safety, scale, storage, and space for all phases of development.

Infants.

Early childhood is a time of innocence and wonder, warmth and exploration. A child's room must therefore provide both security and stimulation as well as create fond memories. It is a place that must function efficiently and hygienically for the care of the newborn. The most important design of all for children, however, is the one that connects them to the family. Sandra Edwards, founder of CHILDESIGN, says that "appropriate design is about creating a support system," not a primary-colored playpen. The standard misconception is that designing for children is about surface decoration, cute imagery, and a parent's own fantasies of what it's like to be a child. Instead, the most effective environment from birth on calls for simplicity, even neutrality. Babies love brightness. They respond to clear colors, tactile textures, and strong patterns. Color affects them before shape; recognizing patterns is probably a baby's first intellectual activity. That means placing brightly colored or patterned objects—pillows, sheets, toys, and mobiles—within easy view. This preoccupation with brightness lasts; a preschooler will choose a bright red chair over a more comfortable pale-colored one. Don't forget the parents: a comfortable chair is an emotional necessity for them to be at ease too.

According to Sandra Edwards, founder of CHILDESIGN, a non-profit organization committed to improving children's lives and educations through good design, adjusting proportions is a sure way to engage a child both physically and psychologically. But that doesn't have to mean investing in a full suite of miniature furniture. The solution can be as simple as easy-to-grasp pulls added to a bureau drawer containing the child's clothes or toys. Or it might be a small area rug in the living room that the child can identify as his or her own special spot for play amidst adult action. P.S. Make sure it's washable and small enough to move around.

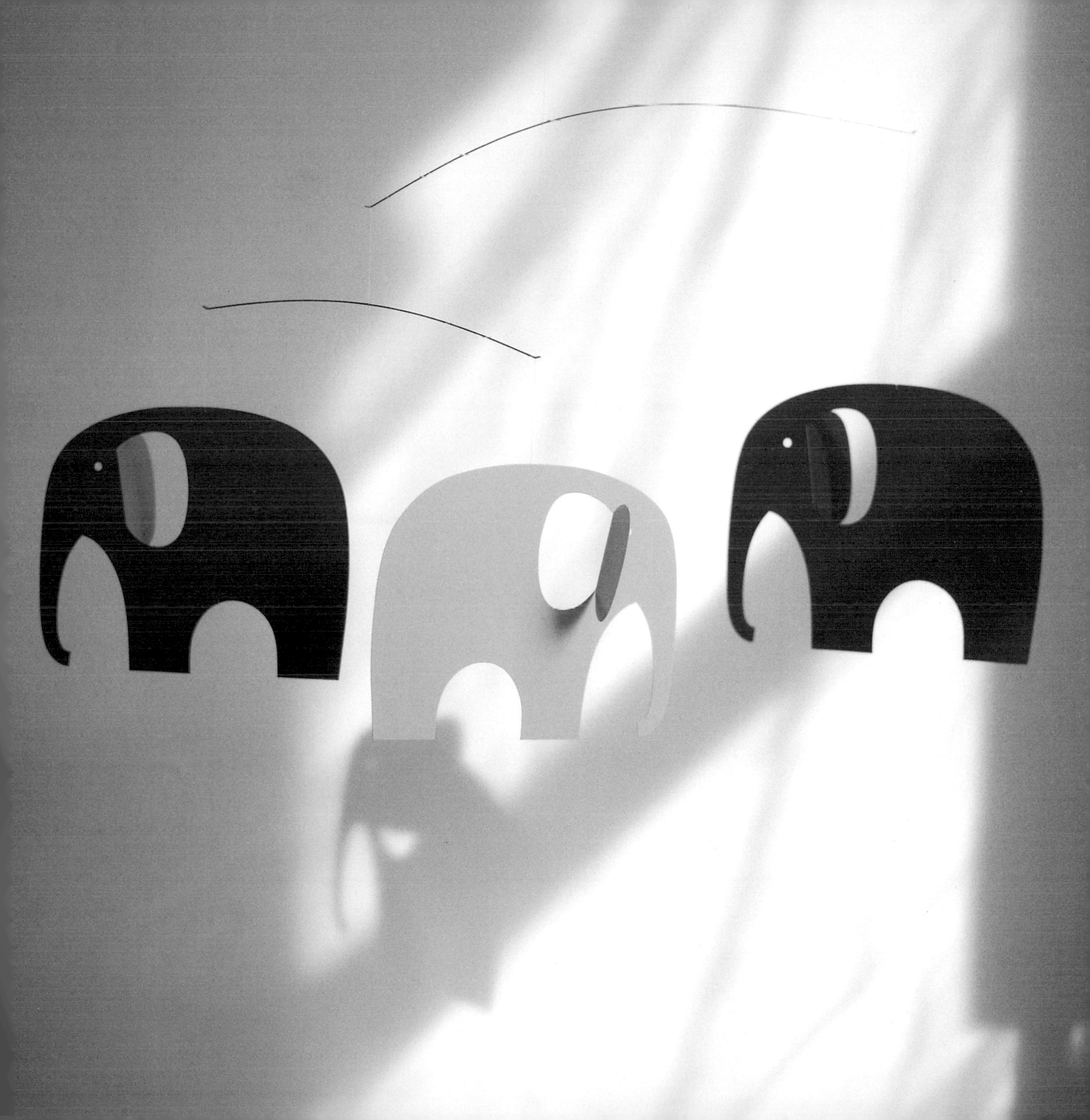

Early years. Without a doubt, children have different opinions on decor. According to the late designer and psychologist Tony Torrice, founder of Learning Environments, talking to children and making lists about their wants and their needs as well as your own helps in finding a design that works. The child will not only feel more comfortable in the room but will have experienced a significant moment in realizing that it is possible to have an

ABOUT THAT RED CORVETTE BEDSPREAD

While a child will instantly grow out of a theme room, there will always be an inventive way to use a window seat, a big closet, or a pitched ceiling. A closet with Dutch doors might become a puppet theater; or a raised platform might suggest a stage for improvised performances. Lighting is also an affordable way to conjure enchantment. Soft night-lights, decorated lamps, lighting by which to play and to read, and plenty of daylight all stimulate a playful imagination. Abundant storage is essential: bins and shelves, pegs and hooks, closets and chests.

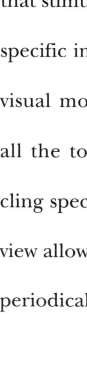

impact on the world. For them, good design isn't defined by aesthetics. It is more about engaging the senses and fueling strong emotions. Style at this age is a sensory experience spun out in the imagination and nourished by spaces that stimulate without dictating specific imagery. Instead of the visual monotony of displaying all the toys all the time, recycling specific toys in and out of view allows younger children to periodically rediscover them.

T e e n s . If design in a teen's room typically appears to be chaos incarnate, it is in fact the very picture of coming to grips with self-discipline. Young children at home like to explore and test the kind of power they have within the family; the teenager must strike out and achieve an identity in society. Balanced on the threshold between home and the world, influence his or her surroundings in a graphic way: rearranging the furniture, selecting colors, making room for collections. These are ways that an adolescent can invest in caring for a space. From horseback-riding ribbons to celebrity photographs, collections also foster self-expression. Ample wall space should be available for their display.

"I like both kinds of people with blue hair."

PENN JILLETTE, *of Penn & Teller*

teenagers are not only confronted with a craving for independence but for reassurance, too. The standard reaction of parents is nervous supervision, whereas it should be gentle buffering. The teen's room is more like a scratch pad than a blank canvas. Experiments may backfire, and so flexibility is more important than ever. The adolescent needs to be allowed to The refrain of youth always seems to be "leave me alone." As at any age, their privacy needs should be acknowledged and respected, not feared or considered an offense. Now more than ever, the community can help where individual parents cannot. As they experiment with different identities, adolescents seek mentors and need role models.

VOICE OF WISDOM

Christopher Alexander

(b. 1936). A mathematician as well as an architect, a contractor, and a craftsman, Christopher Alexander is best known as a philosopher and a teacher. Since the Sixties, Alexander has rejected the standardized methods and style obsessions of the architectural profession in favor of designs that are both more humane and responsive to the environment. For Alexander, the very ugliness of the contemporary built world attests to our alienation from a natural and harmonious way of building. And he has staked his career on finding a different way to build.

In 1967, Alexander founded the Center for Environmental Structure at the University of California, Berkeley, where he teaches, to analyze the role of design in fostering a sense of community and individual well-being. In his writings, particularly *A Pattern Language* and *The Timeless Way of Building*, Alexander speaks eloquently of good design as something that people understand emotionally more than intellectually. *A Pattern Language* describes 253 design "patterns" ranging from public transportation engineering to a farm kitchen inglenook.

This soft-spoken iconoclast has been rebuffed by some as too spiritual but championed by others, among them Prince Charles, as an inspired reformer. Several recently completed buildings put Alexander's philosophies into practice. They include a college campus and housing project in Japan and a homeless shelter in San Jose, California. Alexander believes, above all, that architects must take seriously their role as custodians of harmony in the built world.

ICONS OF INFLUENCE

stones
leopards
Rumford fireplaces
alcoves

English universities
courtyard houses
Italian hill towns
Greek villages
Oriental temples

"Style which is not connected to rea

BIBLIOGRAPHY

Community and Privacy: Towards a New Architecture of Humanism, 1963; *Notes on a Synthesis of Form*, 1964;
A Pattern Language (Alexander et al.), 1977; *The Timeless Way of Building*, 1979

INTERIOR DESIGN

" 'Decor' and the conception of 'interior design' have spread so widely, that very often people forget their instinct for the things they really want to keep around them."

DOORS

"The success of a room depends to a great extent on the position of the doors. If the doors create a pattern of movement which destroys the places in the room, the room will never allow people to be comfortable."

ARCHITECTURE

"Stones arc what architccture really is."

BEAUTY

"What does 'beautiful' mean? It means that the thing makes me feel joyous, more rooted in the world, more whole as a person."

human feelings is entirely fictitious."

E l d e r s. At the end of the twentieth century, it's clear that more primitive tribes than ours have been far more sophisticated in taking advantage of their elders. Our segregation of age groups in the name of progress has left little in its wake but alienation.

The needs of the elderly are special, but not so extraordinary that they must be removed from the community into isolated facilities. In terms of social involvement, elders should be part of a group but not responsible for it. These are the years when privacy can too easily slide into solitude, and solitude into deprivation. In terms of design, older people are dealing specifically with maintaining their environmental competence. For instance, an older person will feel more in control in a small room crowded with many things than in a large one, especially when the surrounding objects reinforce their personal history. Unusual as it sounds, hard-to-reach items should be left where they have always been.

VISUAL CONTROL

For an elderly person, visual control translates into decor that is not full of busy patterns or highly reflective surfaces. Vivid and solid color contrasts enhance visibility. Red, orange, and yellow appear as more distinct than blue, violet, or green.

COMFORT

Place firm pillows at the back of a chair from which it's difficult to rise, or put foam padding beneath the upholstered cushion of an especially deep armchair. For a chair that's too soft, put a piece of plywood under the seat cushion.

It's often easier for an elder to accommodate physical exertion than to remember where something has been moved. Carefully placed personal effects may help prevent disorientation and even memory loss.

Memory, in many ways, plays the central role in making an elder person's space truly habitable. As sociologist Sandra Howell has written, elders are keenly aware of their former status in the world and use memory to redefine, or "reweave," their pasts. The home in this case is a source of self-esteem; and decoration itself serves as a graphic metaphor for life history. A septuagenarian widow who no longer needs her massive Chippendale dining set will refuse to remove it. As far as she's concerned, it's tangible and recognizable proof of her importance.

In place of the inevitable pull of mortality, elders connected to families and to their community can become guardians and mentors to their young, passing on valuable lore and, for themselves, preparing not for death but continuity.

"We shape our dwellings and afterwards our dwellings shape us."

WINSTON CHURCHILL

WHOLE HOUSE

"What is the use of a house
if you don't have a decent planet
to put it on?"

HENRY DAVID THOREAU, *Walden*

"As much energy leaks through American windows each
year as flows through the Alaskan pipeline."

The Green Lifestyle Guide

Taking care of the environment starts at home. And recycling is only the beginning. There are a multitude of other considerations with direct bearing on the home: energy conservation, toxic chemicals, and endangered trees are just a few. Much of "going green" at home is based on plain common sense. From stopping your junk mail to installing solar energy panels, it's the gestures both big and small that when multiplied by thousands will literally make a world of difference. And if at times the odds seem overwhelming and the options bewildering, remember the four "R's": Reduce, reuse, recycle, and reject. Consider the following general areas when thinking about the Whole House. The degree to which you adapt is a matter of personal preference to suit your own patterns of living.

Household Toxins.

There's chemical warfare going on under the kitchen sink, and it has been making people sick. Now that modern construction and energy-efficient practices guarantee that houses are more airtight than ever, it's essential to give no quarter to the innumerable chemicals and treated materials that give off toxic fumes. Trapped inside, they will contribute to "sick house" syndrome. The first step in getting control of the problem is learning to read labels. Watch out for anything that may be hazardous, toxic, or harmful, and start looking for substitutes.

TRY SUBSTITUTING

Cedar blocks or dried lavender for mothballs, which contain toxic formaldehyde

A shallow dish of ammonia for oven cleansers. (Ammonia should loosen carbon deposits, especially when left in the oven overnight. Wash off with hot soapy water.)

Water-, plant-, or mineral-based paints for oil-based paints

Vinegar for fabric softener. It also cuts mildew and wax build-ups. Use it as a room freshener that absorbs odors.

Half a lemon dipped in borax for scouring instead of an abrasive powder

THE COMMON SENSE SOLUTIONS

Doors: Keep doors to unused rooms shut and their temperature at 55 degrees when unoccupied in winter. **Water:** Fill a basin with warm water for hand-washing dishes, then rinse with cold water. (Cold water leaves crystal glasses spot-free.) **Washing:** Only run full loads of laundry in the washing machine and dishes in the dishwasher. **Clothes:** Recycle old clothes into rags instead of using paper products. **Plastics:** Reuse plastic margarine and yogurt containers for refrigerator storage. **Spray cans:** Buy products in pump dispensers, not aerosol cans. **Cups:** Recycling starts at breakfast. Keep a mug handy at home, work, or on the road to avoid disposable and styrofoam cups. Styrene, a hazardous chemical that makes up styrofoam, tends to leach into liquids, especially when hot or slightly acidic, such as tea with lemon. **Soap:** Save those annoying last scraps of soap in a bottle. Add water to dissolve into dish liquid.

TOXIC PRODUCTS: Chemical abrasives; chlorine bleach; disinfectants; drain, rug, oven, and toilet cleaners containing halogenated hydrocarbons; mothballs; oil-based paints, strippers, and thinners; phosphates; silver polish

INDOOR POLLUTANTS: Air fresheners; dry-cleaned clothes in plastic bags; formaldehyde-based building materials; gas appliances and heaters; pesticides; scented products; synthetic fibers and finishes

Avoiding certain cleansers doesn't have to mean leading a life of grime. It's true that natural cleansers usually take more effort for not always perfect results. However, in the last few years, companies such as Seventh Generation have worked hard to locate the most effective alternatives and bring them to the market for consumers.

Bleached white coffee filters are banned in Sweden. 80% of all garbage ends up in landfills; 10% is recycled; 10% is incinerated.

A serious radon leak is the approximate equivalent of smoking two packs of cigarettes a day.

Energy.
Energy is a luxury we can no longer afford to waste. According to population analysts, in 1990 the average American energy consumption was equivalent to that of 3 Japanese, 6 Mexicans, 13 Chinese, 35 Indians, or 499 Ethiopians. Even a little applied conservation and recycling on the home front has the potential for substantial environmental benefits and even financial savings. In fact, the implementation of energy conservation techniques in America since 1973 has knocked $150 billion per year off the national energy bill.

Recycling.
Reject, reduce, reuse, recycle. The 4 R's are a mnemonic device that gets right to the point of the recycling process at home: Reject excessive packaging; reduce reliance on plastics; reuse containers wherever practicable; recycle paper, glass, and aluminum. While thoughts of trying to save the planet often seem too overwhelming for the average citizen even to contemplate, recycling is something that every individual can grasp and act on. It's also a notion that lends itself to today's most effective (for better and for worse) social movers—i.e., commercial marketing agents.

DROUGHT DEFENSE. Install a water filter, low-flush toilets, aerator faucet heads. Take showers, not baths.

LIGHT BULBS. An 18-watt compact fluorescent screw-in bulb uses 75% less electricity, lasts ten times longer than a 75-watt incandescent bulb, and saves $40 to $60 over the bulb's lifetime.

DRYERS. Electric dryers use 1,000 kilowatt-hours of energy a year. Use a clothesline or drying rack instead.

INSULATION EFFICIENCY. The chief dilemma in insuring an energy-efficient and healthy house is that the former condition calls for airtight insulation to maximize the energy output of both heaters and air-conditioners. A healthy house, however, needs to breathe, and ample fresh-air circulation is an absolute requisite. The solution is to bring air-flow patterns under control by sealing all incidental air leaks and then relying on well-placed windows, vents, and doors to maintain and direct the most effective circulation.

NEW TECHNOLOGIES. Brave new technologies now in development for commercial feasibility include photovoltaic (PV) cells and desiccant air-conditioners. PV cells translate direct sunshine into usable electricity. Incorporating the cells into roof tiles would allow for a constant and reliable energy source at no expense to the environment. Desiccant air-conditioners based on water, not ozone-depleting chemicals, involve a technology remarkably similar to the way in which the human body cools itself through surface evaporation.

PACKAGING WASTE. By weight, 30% of the garbage in national landfills is packaging.

PAPER VS. PLASTIC. It takes an industrial-sized plastic bag full of leaves at the dump 200 years to degrade. "Wet-strength" heavy kraft paper bags can withstand two weeks of rain on the curb, and are fully recyclable.

NEW-OLD TRENDS in recycling means back to the way things used to be done: string bags for shopping, rechargeable batteries, cloth diapers, composting at home

ENERGY SAVERS

Compact fluorescent bulbs last longer and use far less electricity than standard tungsten bulbs.

Replace paper products with washable cloth: use table napkins, dish towels, and handkerchiefs, and then reuse them as rags.

Old-fashioned fans are more elegant and energy-sensitive than air-conditioners for cooling down rooms.

Hanging your clothes out rather than tossing them into the dryer saves a great deal of energy.

F u r n i t u r e . It isn't at first obvious how furniture fits into the environmental debate. Think again—about wood from endangered trees. Many manufacturers have already limited their use of rare mahogany, teak, and other tropical species that are the hallmark of good furniture but that also cannot easily be grown as a sustainable crop. There's even more at stake. In the United States, furniture manufacturing is responsible for 1% of all industrial, ozone-depleting VOC (volatile organic compound) emissions. Closer to home, many finishes and furniture-making processes rely heavily on formaldehyde-based chemicals whose poisonous fumes will continue to reek (or "out gas") in the home for the life of the piece.

B u i l d i n g . Look to the past for the best ideas in home designs that work with, instead of against, nature. Vernacular architecture was born of the necessity to inhabit the landscape economically, efficiently, and simply. While old houses may often appear to us now as impossibly quaint, they are often full of ingenious designs for taking the best advantage of local materials and climates. From the so-called widow's walk that served to bring cool air and light into the dark heart of New England homes to the broad verandahs that shade the adobe ranches of Texas or the Charlestown town houses angled to catch a breeze, regional architecture offers not only practical, but beautiful design solutions.

OLD-GROWTH VS. SECOND-GROWTH FORESTS. "Old growth" is the term applied to trees from our most ancient forests, including Douglas fir, redwood, and red cedar. In North America, only 5% of old-growth forests remain intact. While the enduring properties of many old-growth trees—redwood resists rot; cedar repels water; fir is strong—make them ideal for construction, conservationists advocate using second-growth trees grown in plantations, or even salvaged old growth.

ENDANGERED SPECIES: mahogany, teak, rosewood, liana, ebony, redwood, cedar

SUSTAINABLY GROWN SPECIES: apple, beech, birch, walnut, elm, oak, pine, spruce, poplar

FURNITURE-MAKING CHECKLIST
(a few questions to ask when shopping for new furniture):

What kind of foam was used? Cushion foams made with compound urethane are toxic. Ask for CFC-free foam. To replace foam, some companies are returning to older technologies, such as cotton-wrapped springs and horsehair stuffing.

What about toxic glues and adhesives? Instead of formaldehyde-based adhesives, buy furniture held together with water-based polyvinyl acetates (PVAs).

Is the finish water-based?

Remember that old furniture didn't take advantage of modern technologies or chemicals. Made of solid woods, possibly even hand-made, they are almost always free of toxins.

Formaldehyde, or urea-formaldehyde, is common in most cabinets and shelving made from plywood, particle board, and composite woods. When using plywood, either request the slightly less processed exterior grade or seal the plywood with polyurethane or AFM water-seal. Reject pressure-treated woods commonly sold as deck material, because they contain wood preservatives known to cause cancer.

"A four-foot stack of recyclable newspapers saves the life of one tree." *Ecologue*

Awnings, porches, trellises, and pergolas shade southern exposures and cool the air as it enters the house.

Placing windows on opposite walls but not directly across from each other forces air to circulate more actively. The laws of physics say that hot air rises, so it's always a good idea to juxtapose low windows to windows or vents placed as high as possible, thus drawing cool air in and letting hot air escape above.

WAYS TO INCREASE AIRFLOW

Interior windows,
transoms over
doors, cupola or
ceiling vent,
French doors,
cathedral ceilings
with fans,
a fan at the top
of the stairs,
pitched-roof porches

"The New Chair" from Domestic Furniture is down-filled with cotton batting instead of being stuffed with foam. The upholstery is 100% wool, and the wooden legs are made of maple or cherry, two hard woods in abundance in the United States.

Insulation for modern houses long relied on asbestos, now a proven hazardous material. Experiments in new insulators have ranged from using recycled computer paper and newspapers to volcanic pumice stone.

Sun rooms are most effective at collecting heat when positioned 30 degrees off true South.

"To me air-conditioning is a dangerous circumstance. The extreme changes in temperature that tear down a building also tear down the human body."

FRANK LLOYD WRIGHT

WHERE

At the very heart of CHIC SIMPLE is one basic premise: accessibility. People should be able to locate easily the furniture, objects, and services they need to make a home. To that end, the following resource listings are as encompassing as possible, including flea markets and mail-order catalogues as well as department stores, boutiques, and consulting services. Unless otherwise noted, all international listings indicate stores that sell contemporary furnishings and modern classics. Stores with multiple locations appear alphabetically under the National heading.

CALIFORNIA

ALBRO SISAL
8807 Beverly Boulevard
Los Angeles, CA 90048
213/274-0671
(floor coverings)

BOYD LIGHTING
56 Twelfth Street
San Francisco, CA 96103
415/431-4300
(residential and contract lighting)

CHAMBERS
P.O. Box 7841
San Francisco, CA 94120
800/334-9790
(mail-order bed and bath products)

THE DINING ROOM SHOP
7645 Girard Avenue
La Jolla, CA 92037
619/454-8688
(tablewares)

DOMESTIC FURNITURE
7385 Beverly Boulevard
Los Angeles, CA 90036
213/936-8206
(home furnishings)

FRED SEGAL FOR A BETTER ECOLOGY
420 Broadway
Santa Monica, CA 90401
310/394-6448
(eco. department store)

MODERN LIVING
8125 Melrose Avenue
Los Angeles, CA 90046
213/655-3898
(contemporary furniture)

NEW STONE AGE
8407 West Third Street
Los Angeles, CA 90048
213/648-5969
(modern objects and furnishings)

REAL GOODS
966 Mazzoni Street
Ukiah, CA 95482
800/762-7325
(mail-order environmental products)

TANYA HOVNANIAN
5117 West Adams
Los Angeles, CA 90016
213/936-3536
(decorative objects, wrought-iron lights)

WICKER WORKS
267 Eighth Street
San Francisco, CA 94103
415/626-6730
(woven furniture)

COLORADO

HOSEK MANUFACTURING COMPANY, INC.
4877 National Western Drive
Denver, CO 80216
303/298-7010
(plaster and fiberglass moldings)

CONNECTICUT

GREY & CO. DESIGN CONSULTANTS
604 North Street
Greenwich, CT 06830
203/869-8479
(specializing in kitchen design)

DELAWARE

THE AFFORDABLE ANTIQUE MALL
4300 Highway 1
Rehobeth Beach, DE 19971
302/227-7914
(antiques)

FLORIDA

ARANGO
7519 Dadeland Mall
Miami, FL 33156
305/661-4229
(*Euro-style furnishings*)

THE GALLERIA
2384 East Sunrise Boulevard
Ft. Lauderdale, FL 33304
305/563-6688
(*contemporary Italian furnishings*)

GEORGIA

DOMUS
1214 Perimeter Mall
4400 Ashford-Dunwoody Road
Atlanta, GA 30346
404/396-1064
(*modern Italian furniture*)

ILLINOIS

DECORATORS SUPPLY CORP.
3610 South Morgan Street
Chicago, IL 60609
312/847-6300
(*moldings, brackets, fireplace mantels*)

ELEMENTS
738 North Wells Street
Chicago, IL 60610
312/642-6574
(*home accessories and furnishings*)

IMPULSE
261 East Market Square
Lake Forest, IL 60045
708/234-0709
(*home accessories and furnishings*)

LUMINAIRE
301 West Superior
Chicago, IL 60610
312/664-9581
(*classic and contemporary European furniture,
lighting, and accessories*)

ORBIT DESIGN INC.
4147 West Ogden Avenue
Chicago, IL 60623
800/458-4147
(*home accessories and furnishings*)

**RICHARD HIMMEL DESIGN
PAVILION**
219 West Erie Street
Chicago, IL 60610
312/266-0002
(*Art Nouveau and Art Deco furniture*)

SALVAGE ONE
1524 South Sangamon Street
Chicago, IL 60608
312/733-0098
(*architectural artifacts*)

INDIANA

WEBBS ANTIQUE MALL
200 West Union Street
Center Village, IN 47330
317/855-5542
(*antiques*)

LOUISIANA

MARIO VILLA GALLERY
3908 Magazine Street
New Orleans, LA 70115
800/783-8003
(*neoclassical metal furnishings*)

MAINE

THOS. MOSER
72 Wright's Landing
P.O. Box 1237
Auburn, ME 04211
207/784-3332
(*hand-crafted furniture*)

MARYLAND

**SMART HOUSE LIMITED PART-
NERSHIP**
400 Prince Georges Boulevard
Upper Marlboro, MD 20772
800/759-3344
(*Smart House information*)

MASSACHUSETTS

MOHR & MCPHERSON
290 Concord Avenue
Cambridge, MA 02138
617/354-6662
(*handcrafted accessories and furnishings*)

THE RENOVATOR'S SUPPLY
Renovators Old Mill
Millers Falls, MA 01349
413/659-2231
(*mail-order plumbing and hardware*)

SHAKER WORKSHOPS
Box 1028
Concord, MA 01742
617/646-8985
(*Shaker reproductions*)

MISSOURI

**GAINSBOROUGH HARDWARE
INC.**
P.O. Box 569
Chesterfield, MO 63017
314/532-8466
(*custom brass, porcelain, stone doorknobs*)

NEW HAMPSHIRE

GOOD AND CO.
Salzburg Square Route 101
Amherst, NH 03021
603/672-0490
(stenciled floorcloths)

NEW JERSEY

ORAC DECOR OUTWATER PLASTICS
4 Passaic Street, Dock Number 1
Woodridge, NJ 01775
800/888-0880
(polyurethane moldings)

POP KORN
4 Mine Street
Flemington, NJ 08822
908/782-9631
(Depression glass and pottery)

SALLY GOODMAN ANTIQUES
North Union Street
Lambertville, NJ 08530
609/397-3883
(elegant country furnishings and furniture)

NEW MEXICO

LIVOS PLANTCHEMISTRY
614 Agua Fria Street
Santa Fe, NM 87501
800/621-2591
(100% natural paints, finishes, stains)

MCMILLAN'S WOODWORKS
1326 Rufina Circle
Santa Fe, NM 87501
505/471-4934
(handcrafted Southwest-style furniture)

TAOS FURNITURE
232 Galisteo Street
P.O. Box 2624
Santa Fe, NM 87504
505/988-1229
(handcrafted fine furniture)

NEW YORK

ABC CARPET & HOME
888 Broadway
New York, NY 10003
212/473-3000
(antique, reproduction, and contemporary furnishings)

AD HOC SOFTWARES
410 West Broadway
New York, NY 10012
212/925-2652
(home accessories)

ALAN MOSS
88 Wooster Street
New York, NY 10012
212/219-1663
(Art Deco and Fifties furniture)

ARCHITECTURAL SALVAGE WAREHOUSE
337 Berry Street
Brooklyn, NY 11211
718/388-4527
(architectural artifacts)

ARONSON'S CARPET & TILES
135 West 17th Street
New York, NY 10011
212/243-4993
(floor coverings)

ARTISAN ANTIQUES
81 Waverly Place
New York, NY 10003
212/353-3970
(Art Deco furnishings)

B & J FABRICS
263 West 40th Street
New York, NY 10018
212/354-8150
(contemporary fabrics)

BERTHA BLACK ANTIQUES
80 Thompson Street
New York, NY 10012
212/966-7116
(antiques)

BLUMENTHAL, INC.
979 Third Avenue
New York, NY 10022
212/752-2535
(textiles, wall coverings, furniture)

CHILDESIGN
17 East 70th Street
New York, NY 10021
212/734-4149
(childhood environment consultants)

CRAFT CARAVAN
63 Greene Street
New York, NY 10012
212/431-6669
(African tribal furniture)

DAKOTA JACKSON
306 East 61st Street
New York, NY 10021
212/838-9444
(contemporary furniture)

DELORENZO 1950
965 Madison Avenue
New York, NY 10021
212/535-8511
(French and Italian Fifties furniture)

DEPRESSION MODERN
135 Sullivan Street
New York, NY 10012
212/982-5699
(Art Deco and Moderne furniture)

DIALOGICA
485 Broome Street
New York, NY 10012
212/966-1934
(contemporary furnishings)

DIDIER AARON
32 East 67th Street
New York, NY 10021
212/988-5248
(18th- and 19th-century antiques)

E. J. AUDI
160 Fifth Avenue
New York, NY 10010
212/337-0700
(reproduction Arts & Crafts furniture)

FELISSIMO
10 West 56th Street
New York, NY 10022
212/956-4438
(environmental house products and gifts)

FIFTY/50
793 Broadway
New York, NY 10003
212/777-3208
(Fifties and modern classic furniture)

FORTHRIGHT
280 Mott Street
New York, NY 10012
212/334 8291

GEORGE SMITH
73 Spring Street
New York NY 10012
212/226-4747
(updated traditional furniture)

GREAT AMERICAN SALVAGE CO.
34 Cooper Square
New York, NY 10003
212/505-0070
(architectural salvage)

ICF, INC.
305 East 63rd Street
New York, NY 10021
212/750-0900
(modern classics)

JONAS
44 West 18th Street, 10th floor
New York, NY 10011
212/685-5610
(upholstered furniture)

JUST BULBS
938 Broadway
New York, NY 10010
212/228-7820
(all types of light bulbs)

JUST SHADES
21 Spring Street
New York, NY 10012
212/966-2757
(lamp shades)

KNOLL INTERNATIONAL
105 Wooster Street
New York, NY 10012
212/334-1500
(modern classics)

KRAFT HARDWARE
306 East 61st Street
New York, NY 10021
212/838-2214
(decorative hardware and bath fixtures)

L. & J. G. STICKLEY
1 Stickley Drive
P.O. Box 480
Manlius, NY 13104
315/682-5500
(reproduction Arts & Crafts furniture)

LE PETIT TRIANON
1270 Third Avenue
New York, NY 10021
212/472-1803
(European fabrics)

LOST CITY ARTS
275 Lafayette Street
New York, NY 10012
212/941-8025
(architectural salvage and lighting)

MANHATTAN MARBLE
267 Elizabeth Street
New York, NY 10012
212/226-4881
(custom marble furnishings)

MARK SHILEN GALLERY
109 Greene Street
New York, NY 10012
212/925-3394
(tribal rugs and textiles)

MIYA SHOJI INTERIORS
107 West 17th Street
New York, NY 10011
212/243-6774
(Japanese furnishings)

MODERN AGE
795 Broadway
New York, NY 10003
212/966-0669
(contemporary furnishings)

**MUSEUM OF MODERN ART
DESIGN STORE**
44 West 53rd Street
New York, NY 10019
800/447-MOMA
*(store and catalogue: furniture and
decorative objects)*

NEOTU GALLERY
133 Greene Street
New York, NY 10012
212/982-0205
(contemporary and European furniture)

NUOVO MELODROM
60 Greene Street
New York, NY 10012
212/219-0013
(Bauhaus and contemporary furniture)

PACE COLLECTION
986 Madison Avenue
New York, NY 10021
212/535-9616
(contemporary furnishings)

PAULA RUBENSTEIN
65 Prince Street
New York, NY 10012
212/966-8954
(American antiques)

PAXWELL PAINTING STUDIOS
223 East 32nd Street
New York, NY 10016
212/725-1737
(decorative painting, murals)

PETER ROBERTS
134 Spring Street
New York, NY 10012
212/226-4777
(Arts & Crafts furnishings)

PORTICO
379 West Broadway
New York, NY 10012
212/941-7800
(bed linens, sheets, and accessories)

SILK SURPLUS
235 East 58th Street
New York, NY 10022
212/753-6511
(discontinued Scalamandre fabrics)

SIMON'S HARDWARE
421 Third Avenue
New York, NY 10016
212/532-9220
(decorative hardware)

TED MUEHLING STORE
47 Greene Street
New York, NY 10013
212/431-3825
(decorative objects, furniture, jewelry)

TEPPER GALLERY AUCTIONS
110 East 25th Street
New York, NY 10010
212/677-5300
(auction house)

TERRA VERDE TRADING CO.
120 Wooster Street
New York, NY 10012
212/925-4533
*(environmental home furnishings and
products)*

TREILLAGE
420 East 75th Street
New York, NY 10021
212/535-2288
(garden ornaments)

TROUVAILLE FRANÇAIS
552 East 87th Street
New York, NY 10128
212/737-6015
(vintage bed linens, by appointment)

TWO EIGHTY MODERN
280 Lafayette Street
New York, NY 10012
212/941-5825
(contemporary and classic modern furniture)

UNIQUE LAMPSHADES
247 East 77th Street
New York, NY 10021
212/472-1140
(custom lampshades)

URBAN ARCHAEOLOGY
285 Lafayette Street
New York, NY 10012
212/431-6969
(architectural artifacts)

U.S.E.D.
17 Perry Street
New York, NY 10014
212/627-0730
(inspired junk shop)

VITO GIALLO
966 Madison Avenue
New York, NY 10021
212/535-9885
(antique decorative objects)

WOLFMAN, GOLD & GOOD
116 Greene Street
New York, NY 10012
212/431-1888
(home accessories)

OHIO

**THE SHERWIN-WILLIAMS
COMPANY**
101 Prospect Avenue
Cleveland, OH 44115
800/321-1386
(paints and stains in colonial colors)

PENNSYLVANIA

ANTIQUE EMPORIUM
818 7th Avenue
Beaver Falls, PA 15010
412/847-1919
(antiques)

**ARCHITECTURAL ANTIQUES
EXCHANGE**
709-15 North Second Street
Philadelphia, PA 19123
215/922-3669
(Art Nouveau, Art Deco furniture)

IRON APPLE FORGE
P.O. Box 724
Buckingham, PA 18912
215/794-7351
(wrought-iron lighting fixtures and ironwork)

TEXAS

EAST AND ORIENT CO.
2901 North Henderson Avenue
Dallas, TX 75206
214/826-1191
(modern classics)

2 WOMEN BOXING
3002B Commerce Street
Dallas, TX 75226
214/939-1626
(stationery and photo albums)

VERMONT

SEVENTH GENERATION
Colchester, VT 05446-1672
800/456-1177
*(mail-order environmental
products catalog)*

176 Battery Street
Burlington, VT 05401
802/658-7770
(store with green products)

WASHINGTON

CURRENT
815 East Thomas Street
Seattle, WA 98102
206/325-2995
(contemporary furniture)

SHAKERS COTTAGE
23730 Bothell Highway Southeast, Suite B
Bothell, WA 98021
206/481-6282
(Shaker reproductions)

WASHINGTON D.C.

AT HOME FURNISHINGS
3811 Porter Street Northwest
Washington, DC 20016
202/537-1234
(contemporary furnishings)

THE GREEN CONSUMER LETTER
1526 Connecticut Avenue Northwest
Washington, DC 20036
800/955-GREEN
(environmental product information)

WISCONSIN

THE COMPANY STORE
500 Company Store Road
La Crosse, WI 54601
800/323-8000
(mail-order bedding and blankets)

**NATIONAL
LISTINGS**

ARTEMIDE, INC.
150 East 58th Street
New York, NY 10155
212/980-0710
(Euro-style furniture)

ATELIER INTERNATIONAL, LTD.
595 Madison Avenue
New York, NY 10022
212/644-0400
(Modern and Euro-style furniture)

BARNEY'S CHELSEA PASSAGE
106 Seventh Avenue
New York, NY 10011
212/929-9000
(imported and contemporary home accessories)

BED, BATH AND BEYOND
620 Avenue of the Americas
New York, NY 10011
212/255-3550
(contemporary home furnishings)

BLOOMINGDALE'S
1000 Third Avenue, 9th Floor
New York, NY 10028
212/705-3182
(home furnishings)

CONRAN'S HABITAT
160 East 54th Street
New York, NY 10022
212/371-2225
(contemporary furnishings)

CRATE & BARREL
646 North Michigan Avenue
Chicago, IL 60611
312/787-5900
(stores and mail-order: furnishings)

HOLD EVERYTHING
P.O. Box 7807
San Francisco, CA 94120
800/421-2264
(stores and mail-order:storage products)

HOME DEPOT
449 Roberts Court Road
Kennesaw, Georgia 30144
404/433-8211
(home furnishings department store)

MACY'S
34th Street and 6th Avenue, 9th Floor
New York, NY 10001
800/45-MACYS
(home furnishings)

PALAZZETTI
515 Madison Avenue
New York, NY 10022
212/832-1199
(modern classics and contemporary furnishings)

POTTERY BARN
100 North Point Street
San Francisco, CA 94133
415/421-7900
(housewares and furnishings)

RALPH LAUREN HOME COLLECTION
867 Madison Avenue
New York, NY 10021
212/606-2100
(home furnishings and accessories)

SAM FLAX WAREHOUSE
233 Spring Street
New York, NY 10012
212/620-3000
(home office products)

SHABBY CHIC
1013 Montana Avenue
Santa Monica, CA 90403
310/394-1975
(slipcovers and furniture)

THE SHARPER IMAGE
650 Davis Street
San Francisco, CA 94111
800/344-4444
(electronic gear)

STOREHOUSE, INC.
2737 Apple Valley Road
Atlanta, GA 30319
404/262-2926
(modern classics)

URBAN OUTFITTERS
4040 Locust Street
Philadelphia, PA 19104
215/387-0373
(contemporary home furnishings)

WILLIAMS SONOMA
150 Post Street
San Francisco, CA 94108
800/541-2233
(stores and mail-order: kitchenwares)

ZONA
97 Greene Street
New York, NY 10012
212/925-6750
(home accessories, imported and domestic)

INTERNATIONAL LISTINGS

AUSTRALIA

ANIBOU
726 Bourke Street
Redfern
New South Wales, Australia
2/319-0655

BIBELOT
445 Oxford Street
Paddington 2021
New South Wales, Australia
2/360-6902

DEDECE
30 Boronia Street
Redfern 2016
New South Wales, Australia
2/552-1177

DESIGN WAREHOUSE
47-51 Camberwell Road
East Hawthorn
Melbourne, Australia
3/525-4192

REMO MAIL-ORDER CATALOGUE
Oxford at Crown Street
Sydney, Australia
8/029-714
(hip general store and mail-order catalogue)

TANGENT
20 Boronia Street
Redfern 2016
New South Wales, Australia
2/698-5088

CANADA

AU COURANT
1100 Queen Street East
Toronto, Ontario
M4M IK8 Canada
416/466-6460

CHATEAU D'AUJOURD'HUI
6375 rue Saint Hubert
Montreal, Quebec
Canada
514/228-4191

PUR ET SIMPLE
Ayers Cliff
Quebec, Quebec
Canada
418/522-3645
(environmental products)

QUINTESSENCE
1657 Bayview
Toronto, Ontario
Canada
807/482-1252

ZIGGURAT
251 King Street East
Toronto, Ontario
Canada
807/362-5900

DENMARK

BEL MARE
Bredgade 24
1260 Copenhagen K, Denmark
33/93-33-70

BOTIUM BELLA CENTER
Central Boulevard
2300 Copenhagen S, Denmark
31/31-51-69

GEORGE KOFOED
Store Kongensgade 59
1264 Copenhagen K, Denmark
33/15-85-44

GREEN SQUARE COPENHAGEN
Stranlodsvej 11B
2300 Copenhagen S, Denmark
31/57-59-59

REKAHN ANTIK
Laderstraede 5A
1201 Copenhagen K, Denmark
31/32-92-15
(antiques)

ENGLAND

ARAM DESIGNS
3 Kean Street
London WC2, England
71/240-3933

AUTHENTICS
43 Shelton Street
Covent Garden
London WC2, England
71/240-9845

CASA BELLA
29 George Street
London W1, England
71/723-8846

CO-EXISTENCE
17 Canonbury Lane
London N1, England
71/226-1653

COLEFAX & FOWLER
39 Brook Street
London W1Y 2JE, England
71/493-2231
(fabrics)

THE CONRAN SHOP
Michelin House
81 Fulham Road
London SW3, England
71/589-7401

CRUCIAL TRADING, LTD.
77 Westbourne Road
London W2, England
81/221-9000

CZECH & SPEAKE
244/254 Cambridge Heath Road
London E2, England
81/980-4567
(bathroom and kitchen fixtures)

DAVID GILL
60 Fulham Road
London SW3, England
71/589-5946

GREY & CO. DESIGN CONSULTANTS
Fyning Copse, Rogate
Petersfield, Hampshire
England
730/821-424
(specializing in kitchen design)

MUJI
39 Shelton Street
London WC2, England
71/379-1331
(generic household products from Japan)

FRANCE

AU BAIN MARIE
8 rue Boissy d'Anglas
75008 Paris
France

CASA LINEA
73 Boulevard Richard Lenoir
75077 Paris
France
43/38-61-61

CLIGNANCOURT FLEA MARKET
Porte de Clignancourt
75018 Paris
France
(flea market)

ÉCART INTERNATIONAL
111 rue Saint-Antoine
75004 Paris
France
42/78-88-35
(classic modern reproductions)

FORMES NOUVELLES
22 Boulevard Raspail
75007 Paris
France
42/22-78-20

INÈS DE LA FRESSANGE
14 Avenue Montaigne
75008 Paris
France
47/23-08-94

L'ARGENTERIE DES FRANCS BOURGEOIS
17 rue des Francs Bourgeois
75004 Paris
France
42/72-04-00
(antiques and kitsch)

L'ECLAIREUR
3 rue des Rosiers
75004 Paris
France
48/87-10-00

NEMO
17 rue Froment
75011 Paris
France
47/55-46-22

READY MADE
40 rue Jacob
75006 Paris
France
42/60-82-25

SERGE HUBERT
12 rue Jacob
75006 Paris
France
46/33-73-14

GERMANY

AEDES
S-Bahnbogen 599
Berlin, Germany
312/55-04

ARNO
Am Savignyplatz
Berlin, Germany
312/90-10

CASA VIVA
Zürichhaus am Opernplatz
Frankfurt am Main, Germany
69/728-550

CUBUS STUDIO + GALLERY
Kantstrasse 141
Berlin, Germany
313/56-57

EXTRA DESIGN
Wielandstrasse 37
Berlin, Germany
324/33-02

GEBRÖDER THONET
Postfach 1520
D-3558 Frankenberg
Germany
6451/5080

INGO MAURER
Postfach 400449
Kaiserstrasse 47
Munich, Germany
89/381-6060
(lighting)

MODUS MOEBEL
Wielandstrasse 27/28
Berlin, Germany
30/882-7381

ITALY

ALCHIMIA
Museum Alchimia
Foro Bonaparte 55
Milan, Italy
2/58-31-55-49

ARFLEX
Via del Babuino 19
00187 Rome
Italy
6/321-9342

ARTEMIDE
Via Margutta 107
Milan, Italy
70/69-30

B & B ITALIA
Largo Corsia dei Servi 11
Milan, Italy
70/55-31

BERNINI
Via Fiume 17
Milan, Italy
47/40-26

CASSINA
Via Durini 18
Milan, Italy
2/76-02-07-45

DRIADE
Via Fatebenefratelli 9
Milan, Italy
657/3001

I LUOGHI DEL XX SECOLO
Casta San Giorgio 2/R
Florence, Italy

SAWAYA & MORONI
Via Manzoni 11
Milan, Italy
80/00-75

STILNOVO
Via Turati 3
Milan, Italy
655/59-57

ZANOTTA
at Rosi Riparato
Corso Garibaldi 97-99
Milan, Italy
2/456-4402

J A P A N

ACTUS
2-19-1 Shinjuku
Shinjuku-Ku
Tokyo 160, Japan
03/350-6011

CASSINA JAPAN
2-9-6 Higashi
Shibuya-Ku
Tokyo 150, Japan
3/3498-9300

FROGDESIGN TOKYO
4-16-7 Takanawa
Minato-Ku
Tokyo 108, Japan
3/3442-5558

IDEE
KUROSAKI TRADING CO.
5-4-44 Minami Aoyama
Minato-Ku
Tokyo, Japan
3/3409-6581

KOSHINO JUNKO DESIGN CO.
6-5-36 Minami Aoyama
Minato-Ku
Tokyo 107, Japan
3/3406-7370

MATSUYA
3-6-1 Ginza
Chuo-Ku
Tokyo 104, Japan
3/3567-1211

SEIBU DEPARTMENT STORE
1-28-1 Minami Ikebukuro
Toshima-Ku
Tokyo 171, Japan
3/981-0111

S P A I N

ATRI
Balmes 427
Barcelona, Spain
3/211-3066

CASA Y JARDIN
Padilla, 21
Madrid, Spain
1/575-9717

GREY
Balmes 23
Barcelona, Spain
3/318-6166

IDEA MUEBLE
Via Augusta 185
Barcelona, Spain
1/411-0945

INDEA MADRID
Paseo de la Habana, 24
Madrid, Spain

S W E D E N

ARTEMA AB
Kammakargatan 9A
S-11140 Stockholm
Sweden
8/14-24-40
(antiques)

EKERÖ MOEBLER
Malmvik/Lovo
Stockholm, Sweden
8/56-03-40-40

INSIDE INREDNING
Sveavä 74
Stockholm, Sweden
8/15-5011

KULANS ANTIK
Skomakaregatan 24B
S-11129 Stockholm, Sweden
8/10-25-23
(antiques)

PIERRE MUNKEBORG
Antik and Inredningar AB
Grev Turegatan 13A
S-11446 Stockholm, Sweden
8/660-90-38
(antiques)

RESOURCES

SPACE

28 **TABLE, SCREEN, AND TATAMI MAT** - Miya Shoji Interiors, Inc.

31 **DUST PAN** - Hanncock Shaker Village Gift Shop, Mass.; **CHAIR** - Elders chair, Shaker Workshop Catalogue

DESIGN

45 **CHAIR** - Arne Jacobsen fish chair, U.S.E.D.; **VASE** - Berndt Frieberg; **VASE** - Fifty/50

51 **KNIFE BOX** - Victorian velvet-covered knife box, U.S.E.D.; **BOWL** - 1950s Danish bowl, Fifty/50; **FABRIC** - B & J Fabrics; **BOOK** - courtesy of Stubbs Books, New York

THE ROOM

56 **TILES** (from left) - Moravian Tile Works; Manhattan Marble; The Bowery Restaurant Used Supply; Aronson's Tile and Carpet

58 **RUGS** (from left) - American Navajo rug 1920s, Kelter Malcé; wool carpet, ABCCarpet & Home; Sisal carpet, 20th-c. Afghan rug, flea market; 19th-c. Caucasian rug, Mark Shilen Gallery

60 (clockwise from top left) - Renovator's Supply; Janovics-Plaza Paint & Wall Paper; Janovics-Plaza Paint & Wall Paper; Ralph Lauren Home

61 **SCREENS** - Fornasetti bookshelf screen, Bloomfields; Eames screen, Palazzetti

64 (from left) - Irreplaceable Artifacts; Urban Outfitters; All State Glass; B & J Fabrics

68 Irreplaceable Artifacts

FURNITURE

76 **CHAIR** - CM Dining Chair by Charles and Ray Eames, Herman Miller

77 **CHAIR AND SLIPCOVER** - Le Petit Trianon

79 **CHAIR** - U.S. late 19th-, early 20th-c., flea market

81 **CHAIRS** (clockwise from top left) - 19th-c. Bow back Windsor, Farmington, Connecticut Outdoor Sale; Charles Eames' DCW, Fifty/50; Aluminum Fireproof, Cleveland, Ohio; Stickley Morris, Forthright; Le Corbusier, Palazzetti; 19th-c. Italian neoclassical, Didier Aaron

85 **TABLE** - by Noguchi, Palazzetti

86 **TABLE** - 19th-c. Northern European pine work table, Evergreen

87 **CANDLE STAND** - Shaker Workshop

90–91 **SOFA** - Shabby Chic

92 **BED LINENS** - 1920s, flea market, Paris, France

95 **SHELVES** - U.S.E.D., New York; **SHAKER BOXES** - Orleans Carpenters

96 **LINENS** - antique linen, Trouvaille Français, ABC Carpet & Home; **CUPBOARD** - Bertha Black

98 **LAMP** - Tizio lamp, Creative Lighting, New York

99 **SCONCE** - colonial revival sconce, Spider Web; **FLOOR LAMP** - 1930s American brushed aluminum, Fifty/50

100 (from left to right) **LAMP** - hammered copper, American Arts & Crafts, As Time Goes By; **LAMP** - by Noguchi, Fifty/50; **WALL SCONCE** - tin 1920s colonial revival; **WALL SCONCE** - flea market; **1880S TIN CANDY MOLD USED AS VOTIVE** - flea market; **HURRICANE LAMP** - Conran's; **1980S HALOGEN LAMP** - Lighting Plus; **AMERICAN BRONZE LAMP**, 1910, flea market

101 (from left to right) **HALOGEN LAMP** - D. F. Sanders; **LAMP** - by Noguchi, Palazzetti; **HOSPITAL OPERATING LAMP** - junk store; **1950s ITALIAN LAMP** - Delorenzo; **TORCHÈRES LAMP** - 1930s American brushed aluminum, Fifty/50

LIVING

109 **TOWEL** - Portico Bed & Bath

112-13 (left to right) **CHAIR** - fireproof aluminum, flea market; **MACINTOSH POWERBOOK** - computer stores; **TABLE** - George Nelson table, Alan Moss; **PLATES AND BOWLS** - 19th-c. Ironstone, Vito Giallo; **SILVER PLATE** - by William Rodgers, The Country Cupboard at the Tomato Factory; **PICTURE FRAME** - On the Bevel; **CHAIR** - by Thonet, 280 Modern

DETAILS

116-17 **HARDWARE** - Irreplaceable Artifacts, Urban Archeology, flea markets, Simons Hardware, Kraft Hardware Inc., U.S.E.D., Baldwin Brass Center

120 (left to right) - flea market; Renovator's Supply Catalogue; U.S.E.D.; Architectural Sculpture Ltd.; Shaker Workshop Catalogue

122 **PILLOWS** - Le Petit Trianon; **CHAIR AND SLIPCOVER** - Upholstery Unlimited

125 all from flea markets and antique shops

MIXING

128 (clockwise from top left) **CHAIR** - Dakota Jackson; **RUG** - "Tra La La" by Christine Vanderhurd; **SMALL LAMP** - 1920s hammered copper, American Arts & Crafts, As Time Goes By; **STEEL TABLE** - Ad Hoc Software; **BED** - 1939 French, Vito Giallo; **SCREEN** - three-panel screen, Paula Rubenstein; **RUG** -

20th-c. Dhurry, Mark Shilen; **CHAIR** - by Harvey Ellis, L. & J. G. Stickley, Forthright; **SCREEN** (steel rolling rack and canvas)- rack from The American Hangar Corp., canvas custom-made at any good canvas shop; **TABLE** - 3-legged metal outdoor café table, Paris flea market; **LAMP** - by Noguchi, Fifty/50; **TABLE** - 1940s, U.S.E.D.

129 (clockwise from top left) **RUG** - 1920s Navajo, Mark Shilen; **LAMP** - American wrought iron with linen shade, The Tepper Gallery; **BENCH** - African wash bench, Craft Caravan; **CHAIR** - Past & Present Shop, Bloomingdale's; **MIRROR** - Victorian brass-plated mirror, Urban Archeology; **RUG** - by Edward Fields, Fifty/50; **STOOL** - 19th-c. Windsor, Farmington Connecticut Outdoor Show; **SCREEN** - French 1900, Cobweb; **MIRROR** - 19-c., American Empire, Triple Pier Antique Show, New York; **CHAIR** - 1890s English hall chair, Tepper Gallery; **RUG** - 1930s Tibetan, Mark Shilen; **DESK** - 1940s Ameliot, by Greta Magnussen Grossman, Fifty/50; **LAMP** - Tizio lamp, contemporary lighting stores

133 **BED** - 1930s French, Vito Giallo; **RUG** - 20th-c., Dhurry, Mark Shilen; **TABLE** - 3-legged outdoor café table, Paris flea market; **LAMP** - Tizio lamp, contemporary lighting stores; **PILLOWS** (on chair) - Mikes Pillows; **PILLOW COVERS** - sewing by Lisa Hammerquist

134 **SCREEN** (steel rolling rack and canvas) - rack from The American Hangar Corp., canvas custom-made at any good canvas shop; **MIRROR** - 19-c. American Empire, Triple Pier Antique Show, New York; **CHAIR** - 1890s English hall chair, Tepper Gallery; **TABLE** - 1940s, U.S.E.D.; **VASE** - 1920s Steuben, Vito Giallo; **RUG** - 1920s Navajo, Mark Shilen

137 **LAMP** - by Noguchi, 1950s, Fifty/50; **PICTURE FRAME** - On the Bevel; **CHAIR** (against wall) - Past & Present Shop, Bloomingdale's; **DESK** - 1940s Ameliot, by Greta Magnussen Grossman, Fifty/50; **CHAIR** - by Harvey Ellis, L. & J. G. Stickley, Forthright; **RUG** - by Edward Fields, Fifty/50

139 **CHAIR** - by Dakota Jackson; **RUG** - 1930s Tibetan, Mark Shilen; **BENCH** - African wash bench, Craft Caravan; **LAMP** - Tepper Gallery; **PILLOW** (on chair) - by Christine Vanderhurd; **CUP AND SAUCER** - Drab Ware pattern by Wedgwood

140 **STOOL** - 19th-c. Windsor, Farmington Connecticut Outdoor Show; **STEEL TABLE** - Ad Hoc Software; **CHAIR** - ribbon-back Chippendale, 1940s reproduction, Lubin Auction; **SLIPCOVER** (on chair) - B & J Fabrics, sewing by Lisa Hammerquist; **MIRROR** - Urban Archeology; **LAMP** - 1920s hammered copper lamp, As Time Goes By

GENERATIONS

157 **MOBILE** - Metropolitan Museum of Art, children's gift shop

159 **BEAR** - by Gund, F.A.O. Schwartz; **PANDA CHAIR** - Mabel's

WHOLE HOUSE

173 **LINENS** - Terra Verde, flea markets, yard sales; **FAN** - Zona

QUOTES

2 **HENRY DAVID THOREAU,** *Walden* (New American Library, 1960).

26 **FRAN LEBOWITZ,** *House & Garden,* Jan. '90 ; **WITOLD RYBCZYNSKI,** *The Most Beautiful House in the World* (Viking, 1989).

29 **TADAO ANDO,** *Japanese Style* (Crown, 1987).

30 ***SHAKER RULE OF THUMB*** by Shaker Hands (University Press of New England, 1975).

32 **LE CORBUSIER,** *Towards a New Architecture* (tr. Praeger, 1927).

33 **BRUCE CHATWIN,** *House & Garden,* June '84.

38 **LE CORBUSIER,** recalled at memorial speech, 27 Aug. '65.

41 **TERENCE CONRAN,** *The New House Book* (Villard Books, 1985).

44 **FRANK LLOYD WRIGHT,** *An Autobiography* (Horizon, 1943).

47 **LEWIS MUMFORD,** *Sticks and Stones* (Dover, 1924).

48 **ETTORE SOTTSASS,** *House & Garden,* Feb. '88.

50 **ANDRÉE PUTMAN,** *House & Garden,* May '88.

53 **CANDICE BERGEN,** *McCall's,* Oct. '91.

61 **CICERO,** *A New Dictionary of Quotations,* selected and edited by H. L. Mencken (Knopf, 1991).

69 **ETTORE SOTTSASS,** *Art in America,* Feb. '88.

75 **TERENCE CONRAN,** *The New House Book* (Villard Books, 1985).

76 **ETTORE SOTTSASS,** *Metropolis,* Oct. 92.

79 **LUDWIG MIES VAN DER ROHE,** *Time*, 18 Feb '57.

85 **MARK HAMPTON,** *House Beautiful,* Aug. '92.

86 **CANDICE BERGEN,** *McCall's,* Oct. '91.

99 **GOETHE,** *Famous Last Words,* Dorsey Scott (Carlton, 1992)

104 **GEORGE HERBERT,** *A New Dictionary of Quotations, selected and edited by H. L. Mencken* (Knopf, 1991); **TONI MORRISON,** *Jazz,* (Knopf, 1992)

107 **TERENCE CONRAN,** *The Bed and Bath Book* (Crown, 1978).

108 **EVELYN WAUGH,** *Brideshead Revisited* (Little, Brown, 1982)

113 **GEOFFERY BEENE,** interview.

130 **ANDRÉE PUTMAN,** *House & Garden,* Oct. '85.

144 **RAY BRADBURY,** "The veldt," 1950.

160 **PENN JILLETTE,** *The New Yorker,* 15 May '89.

165 **WINSTON CHURCHILL,** *My Early Life: A Roving Commission* (Macmillan, 1987).

168 **HENRY DAVID THOREAU,** *Walden* (New American Library, 1960); *Green Lifestyle Guide* by Jeremy Rykin (Owl Books/H. Holt & Co., 1990).

175 **FRANK LLOYD WRIGHT,** *Natural House* (Horizon, 1982).

191 ***SHAKER SONG*** by Shaker Hands (University Press of New England, 1975).

VOICES

(all quotations either confirmed, expanded, or altered by subjects): **ANDRÉE PUTMAN** in interview, October 1992, pp.118–19; **FRANK LLOYD WRIGHT,** *Collected Writings,* edited by Bruce Pfeiffer, Volumes 1 and 2 (Rizzoli, 1992), pp. 62–63; **ELSIE DE WOLFE,** *Elsie De Wolfe: A Life in the High Style* by Jane S. Smith and Diana Vreeland (Atheneum, 1982), and *The House in Good Taste* (The Century Company, 1914), pp.82–83; **FRANK GEHRY,** *L'Architecture d'Aujourd'hui* (Feb. '89), *A+U* (Jan. '86), *Contemporary Architects* (St. Martin's Press, 1980), *Frank Gehry,* edited by Peter Arnell and Ted Bickford (Rizzoli, 1985), pp.42–43; **CHRISTOPHER ALEXANDER ET AL.,** *A Pattern Language* (Oxford University Press, 1977), *Progressive Architecture,* June '86, July '91, pp.162–63.

PHOTO RESEARCH

CONTEXT: (clockwise from top left) courtesy of The Knoll Group; UPI/Bettmann; UPI/Bettmann Newsphotos; The Max Protetch Gallery, New York; Dudley Gray; © Milton Glaser; Julius Shulman, Honorary AIA

DESIGNER SPREADS: **FRANK LLOYD WRIGHT** - courtesy the Metropolitan Museum of Art, purchase, bequest of Emily Crane Chadbourne, 1972 (1972.60.1), installation by the generosity of Saul P. Steinberg and Reliance Group Holdings, Inc.; **ELSIE DE WOLFE** - photograph by Monica Stevenson, courtesy Barry Friedman, Gallery of New York, Ltd; **ANDRÉE PUTMAN** - courtesy Palazzetti, Inc; **FRANK GEHRY** - courtesy of The Knoll Group; **CHRISTOPHER ALEXANDER** - © Mark Darley/Esto

PHOTO RESEARCH: **JANE MARSHING**

'Tis a gift to be simple, 'Tis a gift to be free, 'Tis a gift to come down where you ought to be. . . .

SHAKER SONG

ACKNOWLEDGMENTS

Hervé Aaron of Didier Aaron, Tony Chirico, Lauri Del Commune, Dina Dell'Arciprete, Stephen Earle, Brian Fingeret, Jane Friedman, Lee Friedman, David Gross of GF55 Architects, Morton J. Gross, Joanne Harrison, Patrick Higgins, Katherine Hourigan, Kurt Houser, Andy Hughes, Kent Hunter, Lesleigh Irish, Carol Janeway, Karen Leh, Micheal Leva, David Mann, Anne McCormick, Sonny Mehta, Gene Meyer, Jeffrey Miller, Ted Muehling, Miranda Ng, Peggy Peters, Eric A. Pike, Linda Rodin, Meg Stebbins, Anne-Lise Spitzer, Robin Swados, Robert Valentine, Shelley Wanger, Charles W. Weiss, Esq., Wayne Wolf

A NOTE ON THE TYPE

The text of this book was set in New Baskerville, the ITC version of the typeface called Baskerville, which itself a facsimile reproduction of types cast from molds made by John Baskerville (1706–1775) from his designs. Baskerville's original face was one of the forerunners of the type style known to printers as the "modern face"—a "modern" of the period A.D. 1800.

DESIGNED, ART DIRECTED, AND COMPOSED BY **Robert Valentine Incorporated**
New York, New York

SEPERATION AND FILM PREPERATION BY **NEC, Inc.,**
Nashville, Tennessee

PRINTED AND BOUND BY **R. R. Donnelley & Sons,**
Willard, Ohio